*How to Help*

*Through Understanding*

JOSEPHINE ROBERTSON

## *How to Help Through Understanding*

"With all thy getting get understanding." Prov. 4:7

𝄞

**ABINGDON PRESS**

NEW YORK
NASHVILLE

HOW TO HELP THROUGH UNDERSTANDING

Copyright © 1961 by Abingdon Press

Library of Congress Catalog Card Number: 61-11786

"How to Visit the Sick" is used by permission of Classmate. Copyright The
Methodist Publishing House.

"How to Help in Time of Sorrow" was first published as "How to Help
When Sorrow Comes" in The Christian Herald, October, 1960, and is
copyright © 1960 by Abingdon Press.

"How to Help Through Letters" was first published as "Our Letters Speak
for Us" in Link, March, 1958, and is copyright © 1957 by The General
Commission on Chaplains and Armed Forces Personnel.

With this book the author pays tribute to Vassar College on the occasion
of its Centennial.

SET UP, PRINTED, AND BOUND BY THE
PARTHENON PRESS, AT NASHVILLE,
TENNESSEE, UNITED STATES OF AMERICA

Dedicated to my friends in
the helping professions and to all
those who have shared the wisdom
of their experience to make this
book possible *including*

*Alice Mooradian —*

*with great admiration for
your wonderful work —*

*Jo*

*October 1961*

# FOREWORD

In this age of do-it-yourself thinking, the newsstands and bookstores are overflowing with "how-to" suggestions. It is also an age of religious interest, growing churches, crowded Sunday schools, and a full calendar of weekday activities, but perhaps one do-it-yourself aspect of religion has been neglected. We know that we are enjoined to feed the hungry, clothe the naked, take in the stranger, visit the sick, care for the widows and the fatherless. But, do we know how?

Do we know how to visit an incurably ill patient in a hospital? To bring comfort in a house of mourning? To encourage one who has met tragedy or disgrace? To cut through the clouds of depression? To make a stranger from a strange land feel at home?

With the help of many wise and kindly people, I have prepared this book dealing with the practical side of spiritual living. It has been written with the thought that its chapters may be useful for group discussion as well as for the general reader.

It is my sincere hope that *How to Help Through Understanding* will help.

JOSEPHINE ROBERTSON

# CONTENTS

# 1

# HOW TO VISIT THE SICK

Do you know how to visit the sick—helpfully? If so, you can be a real friend in time of need. Perhaps you can remember how you felt about visitors when you were ill, how you lay listening for familiar footsteps in the long hospital corridor or waiting for the sound of a car stopping outside your house. If you have had these experiences you will also remember how one caller brought a real lift to the spirit and another, whose intentions were just as good, would go away leaving you wearied to the point of tears. What makes the difference?

From the point of view of the nurse, visitors can be a help or a hindrance. They are a help if they treat the patient as they would like to be treated in the same circumstances, but the inexperienced or the insensitive do not perceive how it feels to be weak, in pain, old, or frightened. Most visitors intend to be helpful, but some don't know how.

To begin at the beginning, make sure the visit is in order. This can be done by checking with a relative or a nurse on the floor in a hospital, after first making sure of the hospital visiting hours. If the hospitalization is to be brief it might be better to postpone the personal call until the patient is back at home.

Make the visit short. A nurse suggests that fifteen minutes is usually long enough, sometimes too long. If another caller appears, this is the cue to slip away. It is tiring to have more than one or two people in the room.

If you are not making a social call, but are staying with the patient for hours at a stretch, it helps to have some handwork. The click of knitting needles is a comfortable, rhythmic sound that gives a feeling of company and does away with the need of conversation. This is relaxing to both patient and companion.

Watch your sickroom etiquette. (Nurses feel strongly on this matter.) Don't jostle the bed, sit on it, or stand too close; in fact, don't stand. Many patients become nervous with people towering over them as they lie in bed. Sit down and locate your chair in a place where the patient can talk with the least strain.

Tone of voice is important, with a low quality the most agreeable. Never whisper! If a patient hears someone whispering to the nurse he is apt to become suspicious and worried. Another precaution is do not discuss the patient's condition in his hearing even if he is apparently unconscious. There is no way of knowing how much he may perceive. A minister told of a difficult old lady who, almost miraculously, came back from a coma of several weeks and repeated the things she had heard, both kind and derogatory. As she was a wealthy woman, the comments were of some interest.

The nurses caution too, against discussing the condition of a deaf person or one who has been mentally confused, on the assumption he would not hear. Often such a person catches a few words not intended for his hearing, and they cause him great anxiety.

Another situation, which has to do with hearing, may arise in a two-bed room when one patient has visitors who converse in a foreign language. If they spoke in the other patient's native tongue, he would turn a blank ear and ignore their discussion, but he feels shut out when he cannot understand and may be suspicious that they are discussing him. This should be avoided when possible.

A good visitor is one who comes in good health and spirits. The caller who feels depressed and at low ebb has little to offer.

Try in conversation to be tactful and constructive. All too many visitors greet the patient with "What's the matter?" and when informed, go on to the appalling observation, "Mary Jones had that, and she had a terrible time!" Don't ask what the trouble is. Often the patient would prefer not to publicize his ailment. If the subject comes up, however, be careful not to stress that Dr. X handles the treatment in a very different fashion. The patient's confidence in his own doctor is important.

If a patient is obviously in pain, it may help to say, "Tell me how you are feeling." This gives an opportunity for release and sympathy which is a relief, particularly, as one friend commented "if you have just heard someone report that you were 'resting comfortably.' "

Avoid worrisome news. It is important to remember that

your friend, lying there in a weakened condition, is not the buoyant person who went around the golf course with you a week or so ago. Your near accident on the highway, the problems that have come up in the office, mischief the children got into, are best not mentioned just now. They may linger to haunt the night hours.

For better subjects of discussion, turn to a hobby or special interest of the patient's, possibly new books, a forward looking mention of activities to be shared upon recovery, something beautiful you have seen. Such subjects will linger pleasantly.

Gifts can brighten the patient's day if they are chosen thoughtfully. Books or magazines should be easy to hold. Flowers are a delight to some, but not all. To a few they suggest funerals. It is well to check with family or friend to be sure that flowers will be welcome, and, if so, sometimes it is possible to discover favorite colors or fragrances. It is simpler for everyone if the flowers come already arranged in a container, and they need not be given in quantity. Space is limited in hospitals, and sometimes three lovely rosebuds are more suitable than a massive floral basket.

Books related to hobby interests are welcome. Games or gifts that offer activity might be a good choice for the patient laid up for a long time, not by sickness, but broken bones. Imagination in giving is a transforming quality. One visitor brought her friend an exquisite little sachet, a tiny gift, but one which gave her pleasure. Another sent little nosegays of fresh flowers to pin to the pillow of one who had lost her sight. Sometimes a new lipstick or bottle of nail polish; gay earrings of floral design or Christmas bells, according to season; candy or cookies to offer staff members and guests; an autograph book or an assortment of greeting cards, with stamps will bring special enjoyment.

Mail is important and offers a simple way to show concern for one who is far away or not in condition to receive callers. Again thoughtfulness enters the picture. A nurse mentioned a friend who mailed a government postcard carrying news and good wishes to a patient every day. The cost was only three cents a day, but its value to the patient was great. In letters and cards, as in personal visits, it is important to omit troubles and scandal and stress things "of good report."

There is a special way to offer your services to a sick friend. When a person says, "Be sure and let me know if there is anything I can do for you," the matter usually ends right there. It is a kind thought, and that is all. More is accomplished, however, when a friend appears and says in businesslike fashion, "I've come to do something for you. What shall it be first? Would you like your hair brushed or some errands done?" Perhaps the patient would like some garments taken home for laundering, help with a manicure, some stationery supplies purchased, or some flowers rearranged. When assistance is offered in this way often the patient is relieved of some problem that has been baffling.

There are many more services that can be rendered when the patient is at home. Here a perceptive visitor can find needs without asking. Perhaps the sink is full of dishes, the refrigerator needs defrosting, a once-over with the dust mop is needed to brighten things up, or a load of clothes needs dropping into the washing machine. If the mother of a family is sick tasty dishes for the family are always appreciated, or if the patient lives alone it is thoughtful for friends to come in bringing tempting dishes for luncheon or tea. Nurses find that people living alone and not feeling well often don't bother to fix the right food. They enjoy both the good things brought in and the company.

If the patient is strong enough, a short outing in a car makes a refreshing change of scene—or even, in case of long confinement, asking the patient if you can help him or her across the room to look out the window. As with the blind, it is better, in aiding infirm persons to offer your arm, rather than taking theirs. They know their own needs, and a steady prop of their own choosing increases feelings of adequacy and confidence.

When it is possible, co-ordinate the calls and gifts through the patient's family or a close friend. Too often in times of crisis the sickroom will be crowded with gifts and callers, if they are admitted. Later there may be depressing days when the patient feels forgotten. The excitement is past and the friends have gone on to other things. This can be avoided if one key person keeps a schedule and suggests good days for calling or sending remembrances. Needless to say, the true and good friend is the one who keeps coming during a long pull to recovery.

Remembrances can take a very practical form. One patient found each morning on the breakfast tray a card saying, "Your hospital care today is the gift of ———. Another much appreciated gift is that of the presence of a private nurse during the first day and night following surgery. Arranging for radio, television, or telephone might be a welcome kindness, or the treat of a visit from a beauty operator—available at most hospitals—might cheer both patient and family.

The thoughtfulness which goes into co-ordinated planning will be appreciated as a heartwarming gift in itself. After all, thoughtfulness is the key to a helpful relationship to a sick friend.

We have been discussing constructive ways of visiting those

whose illnesses are temporary, who look forward to recovery. There should be some mention of those other patients whose prognosis is suffering and death. How does one talk to a person for whom death is waiting just around the corner?

A pastor tells me, from years of experience, that there are no rules. Each case is different, and the approach must be sensed. Some patients know and face their true condition; some do not know it; some know it but have not faced it. Some have spiritual serenity. Others feel bitter and cheated.

A letter from a very ill woman appeared in a woman's magazine protesting the articles written by cancer patients whose illness had apparently made them noble and reformed saints. This, she explained, is not really the case, as illness means not only pain, but endless petty discomfort and irritation even with loved ones. Concerning friends Carol Willis wrote:

We embarrass our friends, for Emily Post has provided no rules for conversation with the dying. We know our friends guard their tongues and force us to watch our words even more. Mentioning that we won't be here next year, or even, perhaps, next month is not in good taste. We have to talk about "when the children are grown" or "when this house gets too big for just two of us" because the sensibility of our friends to death will not allow them to face each minute: the fact that of our dying.

We are quite likely to bore our friends with our preoccupation with illness. We are so wrapped up in ourselves we talk too much. For that reason I never bring up my illnness; but if I am seriously asked about it, I am only too glad to talk. It is a great relief to unburden oneself occasionally, to have the fact that one is bearing pain appreciated. One of the kindest acts a friend can do for a dying man is to listen to him. . . . Don't be disgusted with us if we can't produce too much emotion over your problem. Yours will go on, ours won't.[1]

The pastor follows his trained intuition in talking with the very ill, but for those of us who lack his skill it is helpful to orient ourselves first by talking with a close relative, a doctor, or a nurse. Thus we can learn whether a call would be welcome, how long it should be, what the patient knows and feels about his condition, what sort of talk he would find most helpful, and what, if any, gift might be enjoyed. With this preparation and a prayer for guidance we are better equipped to enter a sickroom and bring loving assurance.

If the patient clings to hope, one can say with complete honesty that medicine is constantly opening new doors. If, as in the letter cited, he wants to unburden himself, one can listen. If his thoughts turn to religion, one can speak in those terms. As opportunity offers, the visitor may allude to the lasting accomplishments of the patient—possibly to his fine children. It may be a unique opportunity to speak from the heart some thought which will be of comfort during dark hours. Even if the right words don't seem to be spoken, however, and the conversation afterwards seems pitifully inadequate to the visitor, the simple fact that a personal call was made, when hands were clasped and eyes showed loving concern, may mean more than the spoken words.

[1] "Our Readers Write Us," *Ladies Home Journal*, 1960. Used by permission of *Ladies Home Journal* and Lothrop Marr Willis.

## 2

# HOW TO HELP
# IN TIME OF SORROW

When sorrow comes to the home of someone close to us, how can we help? This is a question that puzzles many people, including a young bride whom we will call Alice.

Soon after Alice and Jim moved into their first little house, the husband of a neighbor died. Alice had never experienced the loss of anyone close to her, and she did not know what to do. She was a rather shy girl and, in the end, she did and said nothing. The result was that the first time she met the widow after the funeral she was so embarrassed she could hardly speak and was afraid to mention the loss for fear of making the neighbor feel her grief afresh. In spite of her very real sympathy Alice felt strained and guilty and tended to avoid contact with the older woman.

Another young neighbor, no better acquainted than Alice, promptly made up a little bouquet of her best roses and left it at the door with a note saying, "We want you to know we are thinking of you. Please let us know if there is any way we can help."

When they met, a few days later, there was no embarrassment. The girl had expressed her concern. The widow said, "Thank you . . . it meant so much to me," and there was a bond of friendly feeling between them.

A third friend of the widow, who had known her for many years, went into the house quietly and straightened it while the widow was away making funeral arrangements. She looked over the food situation and was able to make some suggestions along this line to friends. When she knew the widow was alone she dropped in, ready to listen, if that would help, assisting with plans and sharing the sorrow.

Many people would like to do something to help in such times of grief, but hesitate, not knowing how to go about it, fearing to intrude, uneasy lest they do the wrong thing. This is particularly true in areas where many young couples come and go, and there are few long-time relationships. Certainly there are no invariable rules of etiquette in the event of death, because the situation may vary from the incomprehensible death of a child to the passing of an aged person who is ready to say in simple faith, "Now I lay me down to sleep." There are, however, procedures which have been found helpful. The simplest is that already mentioned, of the practical services which women have rendered their neighbors from time immemorial—help with the household, help in taking over the care of children, seeing that food is in good supply, offering to house out-of-town travelers.

A clergyman of warm insight warned, however, that the taking over of home duties should not be overdone. Because there is a sudden, terrible vacuum following a death, a certain amount of routine activity can be helpful in maintaining emotional control. It may help, too, to have people coming and going—not stiff, formal hat-and-glove calls, but casual, friendly visits by Dick and Dora, who behave in their natural fashion and come to show they care and are standing by.

Sometimes when callers come they are surprised by the seemingly cheerful atmosphere where there may be even laughter. Human emotions cannot stay at an extreme pitch indefinitely. I remember a wise, elderly Negro woman in one home. A caller said to her, "You must feel dreadfully sad."

"Yes," she agreed quietly, "but I did my weeping this morning."

The surge of grief may return again, and often does when least expected, but the sorrowing go along, for the most part, in fairly normal fashion.

How soon to call? Promptly, but with some relation to the intimacy of acquaintance. If the friend does not feel like talking the visitor will be told, and the fact that he came will be appreciated.

In many places the custom is to call at the funeral parlor rather than the home, during hours announced in the obituary notice. Here friends stop in for a few moments, speak to members of the family who may be present, sign their names in a special book, take a farewell look, if they wish, at the one who has passed away, and, particularly if Catholic, pause for prayer. A call before the funeral permits a personal expression of sympathy not possible during the formal services.

When flowers are sent, they brighten the funeral parlor,

bank the casket during the funeral services, and, later, cover the grave. Because many persons, conscious of the great needs of the world, object to the costly "waste" of great floral displays, there is often a request in the obituary notice to omit flowers. This leaves the choice to the judgment of friends. No one is expected to send flowers, but they will not be refused. A funeral without any can be bleak. With too many, it is a costly display that the deceased might have disapproved. Often other channels of giving are suggested in lieu of flowers. Catholic friends appreciate a contribution for a "Spiritual Bouquet," which is subscription to a Mass for the deceased. Jewish friends —unless another fund is mentioned—will appreciate a gift to the memorial fund of the temple of which the deceased was a member.

If the friend who is gone belonged to another race or faith, one need not hesitate to attend the services or to contribute in whatever way is indicated. This personal tribute will be especially appreciated by the family as an indication of the widespread affection and honor in which their loved one was held. Sometimes it happens that, while the funeral parlor is crowded with floral pieces, the home, where relatives and close friends come and go, does not have a single bloom. Sending a few flowers—rosebuds, spring blooms, or some favorite variety—as a personal token to the home can be a thoughtful gesture. A little vase of flowers waiting in the house for those returning from the ordeal of the cemetery can carry an eloquent message of affection.

When friends live far away they may not receive news of a death until many weeks later. It is never too late, however, to write a warm letter of sympathy or to make a memorial contribution to some cause close to the friend's longtime interest, whether a church fund, the Cancer Society, a college building fund, scouting, or CARE. The amount whether small or large will be appreciated. Most organizations notify the family of such contributions.

Young people do not always realize that the very elderly can be hungry for affection in their sorrow. They assume that these older, wiser ones operate on some different plane of living. When the wife of a fine old man in his eighties died many friends came to pay tribute, but a young woman whom he and his wife had enjoyed knowing did not come, and he missed her. Someone dropped a hint, and the girl came in the next morning, put her arms around him, and gave him a kiss. His face lit up; his shoulders straightened; his eyes filled with tears. She got out her handkerchief, and he got out his. "We talked and talked," the girl said later. "We felt so close."

Next in importance to the physical presence of friends is the mail that comes from them. No one who has not suffered a loss can guess how much the cards and letters mean as they come in from friends nearby, across town, or across the world. Sometimes whole facets of character or influence not realized by the family come to light in letters from old friends, associates, or, perhaps, pupils. Some people feel that such letters are hard to write, but they can be very simple, their only requirement to express sincere feeling. Here are three examples:

Dear Helen,

I was so very sorry to learn about Jim. We had been friends since school days and he meant a lot to me. I remember particularly his helping me over some rough spots during our senior year.

It must be a comfort to you to know how much his faith meant

23

to him. You can always be proud of him. Please let me know if there is any way I can help.

Sincerely,<br>Tom

Dear Mr. Smith,

My husband and I want you to know that we are thinking of you during these difficult days. We are glad that we had the opportunity to know your gracious wife. We appreciated her interest in our young family and I, personally, will always remember listening to her teach our Sunday school class when I was a little girl. Please accept our loving sympathy.

Sincerely,<br>Joan Brown

In the case of the tragic death of a child

Dear Jill,

Since I have learned about Betsy, I want you to know that you are in my thoughts and in my prayers. We do not understand how such things can be—at least not now—but I know her bright, lovely spirit will always be part of you. Some way I know that you will have the strength to face the future bravely, and we will look forward to seeing you again when you feel ready.

Affectionately,<br>Em

People are puzzled, sometimes, about sending Christmas cards after a death in the family. One friend told me that after she had lost her husband she received almost no conventional greetings, with their wishes for a "merry holiday," but many religious cards and personal notes. She appreciated this thoughtfulness. However, another widow commented that her Christmas mail had included many of the usual type. "I liked getting them," she told me, "because I know that I must get back to normal living, but it meant a lot when people added a few personal words to the printed cards."

There is something strange and unreal about the days leading to the funeral. There are arrangements to make, messages to send, people to see. And then it is over. Sometimes it seems as though life itself were over. Now comes the time to face the changed tempo of the home and to make plans for the future. Now is the time of the too still house, the empty bed, the vacant place at the table, and the time when friends fall back into the pattern of their own busy lives. So many people, shocked and excited by tragedy, rush to the scene—but soon forget that the loss is an ongoing one. Now is the time for the true friend to stand by.

How? He may drop in during a lonesome evening; by telephoning just to chat; invite the friend to participate in group activities, particularly along lines of special interest such as music, art, or work with children; mention the deceased in natural conversation; listen when there is a hunger to share memories; and realize how difficult are the "first times alone" in former shared activities such as church or club and help to see them through.

People find it sad that their loved ones are so quickly and, apparently, so completely forgotten by others. In my childhood we always spent Thanksgiving with an aunt and uncle. Years later, when she was widowed, my aunt came to our home for Thanksgiving, and in a little note, subsequently wrote, "Thank you for talking about your uncle at dinner." Words of appreciation spoken long after a death can be precious. I remember a beautiful tribute to my mother spoken by one who had known her when he was a young man. He said simply but eloquently, "She left a sweet memory."

Sometimes when a friend meets tragedy it is possible to find a book in which the author interprets a parallel situation. Many young parents meeting heartbreak have been strengthened by reading Dale Evans' *Angel Unaware*.[1] Elizabeth Gray Vining's *The World in Tune* holds a beautiful affirmation for a woman who has lost her husband.[2] There are many such books. Clergymen can make suggestions for appropriate choices, or a member of the staff of a good bookstore will recommend one.

In talking with those in sorrow, two thoughts may be of help: others do care and out of suffering can come the ability to help.

"People are so kind." The exclamation is heard again and again as expressions of sympathy come from unexpected quarters, or "It has been a revelation to me. I never knew how many people cared." This is a strength-giving assurance and one worth emphasizing.

The second point looks to the future. Out of grief can come deepened sympathy, surer understanding. Often the person who can offer the best comfort is one who is acquainted with grief. Sorrow can bear fruit, the fruit of understanding and the resolve to do something for others, such as working for improved medical treatment or opportunities for education. How many useful hospitals, clinics, scholarships, medical research facilities, special schools, and beautiful parks have had their origins in human sorrow! Even small contributions can help further great works of human service.

[1] Westwood, N. J.: Fleming H. Revell Company, 1953.
[2] New York: Harper & Brothers, 1954.

How can we help? There are many ways, but I often think of what a friend told me after she lost her husband:

Thinking back over those days, I appreciated the flowers and the visits at the funeral home, the gifts to the memorial fund, the letters, and all those people taking time to come to the services, but there were other things—the little bunch of flowers left by a child on the doorstep; the young mother across the road who offered to do errands; the friend who called up and said, "I know you have relatives coming and I'm sending over a cooked ham"; the note that came from a stranger saying she understood just how it was. These were the personal, thoughtful things that shone like lights in the darkness.

The answer to Alice's problem is really a simple one. Many feel sympathy for those in sorrow, but these are not aware of the sympathy until it is translated into action. This can range from a large memorial gift to a pan of muffins. There are many, many ways of showing concern, and to the one bereft each expression is precious.

27

## 3

# HELP AND SELF-HELP
# FOR THE NEWCOMER

When Molly married her young engineer she knew, in an unreal sort of way, that his work might mean a good deal of moving around. She had lived in one New England town all her life, surrounded by relatives and friends. When Jim was transferred across the country she found out what it was to be lonely. She was at home with the baby day after day, with only the baker, the laundryman, and canvassers ringing the doorbell. At church no one but the minister spoke to her. The doctor did not seem to take the same interest in the baby as the one "back home." Jim, absorbed in the new job, tried to cheer his wife by saying, "Never mind, hon, pretty soon we'll have more friends than we know what to do with and will wish it was this peaceful!"

His words were small comfort, but the turning point came unexpectedly when a neighbor stopped to chat with her at the market. "What did you like to do before you came here?" she asked.

"Mostly music. . . . I was going to teach and I always sang in the choir."

"Good. You'll hear from me."

A few days later the neighbor called and invited Molly to go with her to a choir rehearsal. While there were still lonely times in the new town, a corner was turned, and Molly began to feel at home and welcome as she met people with congenial interests.

The first move is usually the hardest for a wife who has grown up in an established circle of friends. However, army wives, the wives of engineers, construction workers, and many others who move about, learn that there are attitudes and techniques which help a newcomer fit into a community in a short time. Molly learned these as she went along, setting up new homes for their growing family.

She learned that it is important for an uprooted family to have a warm, happy climate of affection, with shared interests and hobbies that need never be left behind; that hobbies are a great asset because they offer points of contact with new acquaintances; that a sincere church concern is not only a family bond, but is also a great help in becoming part of a community; that, in moving, emphasis for the children should be, not on the friends they are leaving, but on the opportunity to add new ones; that the greatest asset for a newcomer is enthusiasm for the new town.

Even with such knowledge, however, uprooting and resettling are not easy, and few gestures are so long remembered as friendly acts of welcome in a new neighborhood—things as simple as a pitcher of cold lemonade, a hot casserole, or an invitation to coffee.

A much appreciated call is usually paid by the "Welcome Wagon" or representative of a similar organization soon after a new family comes to town. Financed by the merchants, the caller describes the stores, the civic and cultural activities of the town, and tries to orient the newcomer. One such representative who takes her work very much to heart had this to say:

Whether I'm calling on inexperienced young wives or older people, I tell them that times have changed. They mustn't just sit back and expect people to come calling and seek them out. Few people call these days, but there are many ways to get acquainted. If they are interested in church, I tell them to be sure and go, but not take it personally if people don't speak immediately. Perhaps others are new themselves. I say find out what the church offers in your special field of interest and sign up. Go to the YWCA or YMCA and ask for their program of activities. Perhaps they have a Newcomers Club, with nursery care for little children. Read the paper carefully for such notices as little theater tryouts, ski lessons, adult education courses—whatever you are interested in.

Often, if a girl is newly married and not working, I suggest that she take a Red Cross Home Nursing or Gray Lady Course and help at the Blood Bank. Nursing knowledge can be very useful later, and she will make friends now. There are opportunities for people of all ages, and I like to tell the retired couples or older people who are alone about the interesting Senior Citizen program. Sometimes I have run across foreign brides who were very homesick and lonely and have suggested that they volunteer at the International Institute. They find friends there, and often they can help others.

When a new neighbor arrives, drop in promptly—not a formal, white-glove-and-hat call that will make her feel grubby as she emerges from rearranging the storeroom, but a friendly, casual visit to see how things are going and what you can do.

Since she will be happiest among people of kindred tastes, make a point of drawing her out tactfully on the subject of special training, skills, hobbies, or interests. It is easy for a long-time resident to drop a word in the right place—to establish contact, for instance, between a musician and the local symphony, the artist and the local studio group, the Girl Scout leader and the local organization. Where you find common interests, as we have mentioned above, tell her about the activities and offer to take her to a meeting. Do not ask her religion, but rather, ask if she has found a church.

A church group in our community, where there is much coming and going of industrial employees, was discussing experiences both with and as newcomers. On the basis of their experience and observation, they agreed on a few principles:

Don't talk very much about your old home town. Maybe they *did* do things better back in Ashtabula, but the new neighbors couldn't care less. They want to feel that you are glad to be *here* and think it's a wonderful place.

Don't expect to make lifelong friendships in a hurry. Enjoy all new associations but realize that the ones which are durable may be the ones you least expect.

If you are shown hospitality by new acquaintances, reciprocate promptly and don't feel you must wait until the drapes are finished and you can afford wall to wall carpeting.

Don't let people guess you are lonely. Like Anna, in the *King and I*, who whistled to keep up her courage, act happy, and it will help.

Few members of this church group had lived here more than five years. They agreed with the Welcome Wagon caller that much of the effort for happy integration must be made by the newcomer—but then came a revealing roll call. Each person was asked to tell how she happened to be a member of this group. Over and over came the answer, "Because my neighbor asked me to come with her."

So, by a roundabout route, we come to a very important answer to this problem of how to help the newcomer. Ask her to go with you.

An invitation to go along is equally, or even more highly, valued by the young people in the family. While they might shrink from entering a strange group of their contemporaries alone, they would welcome the opportunity to go with someone their own age.

When you do not find much in common with the new neighbor, you can still render a valued service by saying, "There are bound to be a lot things you will want to find out about. If I can help you with any information about doctors or stores or baby sitters, please feel free to call me any time."

When you have a friend moving to a town where she will be a stranger, one of the nicest things you can do is to write ahead to any acquaintances you happen to have there. If you have none, you might write to the pastor of the church of her denomination and to the secretaries of any national organizations to which she belongs, such as the American Association of University Women or YWCA. In each case tell a little of your friend's interests and activities and say you would appreciate any courtesy extended. The results are out of your hands, and nothing may come from this, but often a few minutes of time, thus thoughtfully invested, will yield a personal contact or invitation which may prove the gateway to a pleasant new path.

Perhaps your church can improve its welcome to the stranger. A good example is that told me by a young Jewish woman whose name had been given to the rabbi by her Welcome-Wagon caller.

"We thought it was pretty wonderful," the young woman told me. "Within a week I had a call from a member of the women's organization inviting me to a meeting, and my husband was contacted by the men. As we had no family here, we were asked to spend the Holy Days in private homes. What's more, every service man in the area had a personal invitation of this sort."

In many churches a couple shakes hands with all comers at the door as they enter and with the clergyman as they leave. Another plan is to ask several couples scattered through the congregation to speak to those they suspect are strangers. Usually the minister calls promptly on new families. This courtesy is appreciated, particularly when followed up by contacts from people of similar age and interests.

For the foreign born, friendly contacts can be even more important. The welcome he finds in attending a church service may determine his attitude toward Christianity in America. A smile, a handclasp, an invitation, can carry the message that we are all brothers in the sight of God.

The director of the Buffalo International Institute, which serves thousands of families of many nationalities each year, summed up her long experience with these words:

We should not criticize the newcomer for seeking out groups of his own people in the city where he lives. He comes here as a stranger, unsure of his abilities, without prestige in the new community, struggling with a different language and environment. With his own people he can relax and find sympathy and warmth. This helps him and gives him strength. Here we like to introduce the newcomer to his countrymen, and then, see him participate in intercultural activities. Bit by bit he reaches out into the new life until he takes his place as a citizen.

Introducing a stranger to such a helpful organization—or to a Newcomers Club at the YWCA or YMCA—can help with many problems, not the least of them loneliness.

Foreigners with a language difficulty find that we are apt to shout, as though they were deaf, instead of speaking slowly and clearly. We give unsolicited advice, as the woman in New York who stopped a little Japanese visitor on a rainy day, looked disapprovingly at her white clad feet on their wooden clogs, and said firmly, "You must get yourself some plastic boots. They have them at every drugstore." We ply foreign guests with unfamiliar foods and seem boastful as we take them on whirlwind tours of our new buildings, museums, or waterworks.

It is more helpful to inquire first what they would like to eat, what they would be interested in seeing, if there is anything we can do for them. Stifle that natural impulse to ask, "What do you think of this country?" Everywhere they meet this question, and it may be difficult to answer—tactfully. Try to learn something of the other's country of origin in order to ask intelligent questions. Mention things you admire in his country, whether art, food, building, or care for the aged. Look for common interests. These are small points, but they can make a big difference.

Long-time residents of a community can become so involved

with their own friends and activities that they cannnot sense the loneliness of the newcomer. While there would not be time for extensive social activity with each new acquaintance, it does not take long to establish contact and to make him welcome.

The two things that are most important by way of help to strangers are to put them in touch with activities they will find congenial and to walk with them a little stretch of the unfamiliar road.

# 4

## HOW TO HELP THROUGH LETTERS

What is a letter? "A written message" says the dictionary, but we all know it is more. A few scribbled lines on a sheet of paper can make or break a day. Good news from a certain person will put a glow over everything around us. A letter containing criticism, complaints, and woe could cast a dark shadow on exactly the same day. The absence of the letter we want can give us a hollow feeling of anxiety. We all know how our correspondents affect our outlook, but let's turn this around. How do our letters affect others?

Our letters speak for us. They come close to being a personal visit and are more lasting. They may be treasured for years. They can do many things—bring a message of love to a very special person; bring happiness to a lonely, older person; bring pride and joy to a child; be shared with friends or a hometown paper; carry a message of friendship abroad to people we may never see. We put ourselves in these little envelopes, for better or worse. We won't dwell on the latter, but, since our letters speak for us, we want them to speak warmly and well. How, then, can we make them helpful? Here are a few practical suggestions.

Write regularly to those who depend on your letters. When days are full and energy depleted a postcard lets them know they are not forgotten. Don't put off writing until there is time "to write a good letter." The delay is apt to grow, and it will be harder to think of enough important things to constitute the "good letter." As a friend expressed it, "If I write often, there isn't room for all the things to tell. If I write every six months, I can't think of a thing to say."

Keep a list or memo book of dates to remember—anniversaries, birthdays, and special days in the lives of families and friends. A message coming on the right day can mean as much as a gift, and is, indeed, a gift. Write promptly to congratulate or to sympathize on happy or on sad occasions. This will be remembered.

Acknowledge kindnesses such as gifts, congratulations, introductions, hospitality, or other favors, with a quick line at once rather than a long letter after the friend has begun to wonder if all is well. In acknowledging hospitality it is gracious to single out the things most enjoyed during the visit.

Answer the questions in the correspondent's last letter. The best way to do this is to keep it handy and reread it just before writing. It is frustrating to try to find out something and have the question ignored while the writer discourses on other things.

A good correspondence is more like a two-way conversation than a one-way broadcast.

While any parent knows that a bedraggled letter is ever so much better than none, an attractively written page is as much a compliment as calling in respectable garb. It helps to have a good supply of stamps and neat stationery on hand. Typing, while not regarded as sufficiently personal by some, is easy to read.

In starting a letter, think what subjects and personalities might be of interest to the reader. Do you share an interest in golf, religion, birdwatching, or books? Write in part, at least, about the reader's work or hobbies. Common interests can bridge gulfs of difference in age and circumstance. I know one young man who wrote regularly to his father during a long illness. Since they both are stamp enthusiasts they maintain a lively and delightful correspondence on this subject. News of friends is always welcome.

Ask questions. Some letters are more like pages of a diary than personal visits. I know a girl who received frequent letters from a man absorbed in graduate studies. Each letter went into detail about the work, but the girl was more interested to see how he signed the missive. Travel letters and the mimeographed newsletters sent to the members of large families are apt to fall into the factual class. They fail to inspire many replies because there is not much to answer. To be sure, these accounts are useful in some situations, such as Christmas card enclosures, but they are more appreciated when handwritten personal messages are added.

People like letters that tell about little things—what the baby did, how the roses are doing, how the meeting went, the joke everyone enjoyed, observations and experiences from every-

day living. Just as people cherish a home-town weekly newspaper when they are away in a big city, so they are interested
in little things that give spice and flavor in a familiar setting.

Letters should be "fit to print." Not that they are apt to get
into print, but any letter may travel wide of its mark and fall
in the wrong hands. I knew a young man whose parents were
separated. It was an unhappy situation, but he did not feel
called upon to judge. He was loyal to both, and whenever he
wrote one, he followed this with a letter to the other. Once he
put the notes in the wrong envelopes and sent them off. Both
were returned promptly and rerouted, but the messages were
so kindly that no feelings were hurt.

Criticism, unsavory gossip, exaggeration, and rumor are
dangerous ingredients. Not only could the letter be read by the
wrong people, but its contents might be quoted without discretion.

Keep the tone cheerful. An army private told me about his
bride, who was almost a continent away. "I had to leave just
after we'd moved into our little house, and she had all kinds
of problems to face that she'd never met up with before. But
she writes me everyday," he said proudly, "and never about her
troubles!" He didn't have to explain how much those letters
meant. It shone right in his eyes.

There are some people who seem perfectly agreeable and
cheerful in person, but when they sit down to write a letter
a dam goes out and in a flood of ink they pour out all their
complaints and woes. Many of the troubles they report may
clear up by the time the letter arrives, but the recipient, not
knowing this, can hardly help being depressed. The best rule
is to stress the things that are heart-warming. When there is
serious illness, trouble, or tragedy to discuss, it can be done

factually, with whatever emphasis the writer can find to bring comfort or hope. The knowledge that the writer cares about and is sympathetic with the reader means much. Fortunately, such matters are occasional in most lives, and the correspondent usually has opportunity in his outgoing mail, to send a lift, a chuckle, a message of encouragement and affection.

Remember to write to travelers. It would seem that those fortunate enough to be journeying in interesting places would be having such exciting experiences that our homespun messages would mean little. The fact is that the words "Sorry, no mail today" spoken at a hotel desk can sound as melancholy as the lament of the mourning dove. People away from home are hungry for news and remembrance. A traveler's itinerary can be kept on file, and for writing abroad, a supply of those economical blue air-letter sheets is available at any post office.

Perhaps letter writing in these days of quick transit and long distance dial phones, is a vanishing art. It is surprising to discover how many prefabricated messages are sold on greeting cards—"Thank you for the hospitality," "Sorry, I forgot your birthday," "Best wishes to the new grandparents," and even "Congratulations on the success of your operation." One looks back at the long, philosophical letters of Franklin, Jefferson, and other great men and finds them full of zest for living and learning, along with much interest in the concerns of the recipient. One wonders that there was time to take quill in hand and write so much. Perhaps eventually other means of communication will supplant the need which gave us such treasures as Paul's epistles, but in certain circumstances, what can compare with a letter addressed in a well-loved script? We can all recall circumstances when special letters—perhaps on a Mother's Day when one was alone or just after surgery—meant more than anything else.

For those of any age who enjoy letter writing and would like to spread a message of friendship overseas it is possible to find a correspondent through one of the organizations devoted to this purpose.[1] In addition to their rosters, thousands of requests for American pen friends come each year to the United Nations, the Voice of America, and city libraries. These names are turned over to the appropriate organization in an effort to match them up with Americans of somewhat similar age group and interest. Writing such letters can be a contribution to international understanding because, as one foreign recipient put it, "We can't always believe the big speeches made for policy purposes, but we do believe the description of conditions that we read in letters from friends." One American found that the contents of his letters were made known to almost two hundred people, since his correspondent maintained the only coffee house in a small village.

Experience has shown that when someone starts an overseas correspondence it often becomes a family affair. The children become interested in the children, the parents in the adults. After a while holiday greetings and little surprises are apt to be exchanged, and, in many cases, years later there may be an

[1] Letters Abroad, 45 East 65th Street, New York 18, N. Y. Adults (over 15). Enclosed stamped, self-addressed envelope.

Children's Plea for Peace, World Affairs Center, University of Minnesota, Minneapolis, Minn. Age 8-18. Enclose stamp. Also good for schools, scouts, 4-H clubs, youth groups.

International Friendship League, 40 Mt. Vernon Street, Boston 8, Mass. Any age, but emphasis on students and young adults.

English-Speaking Union, 16 East 69th Street, New York 22, N. Y. Age 9-16. British Commonwealth Countries. Stamped, self-addressed envelope. Give age and hobbies.

*41*

opportunity to visit in each others' homes. These adventures in letters are not only rewarding in themselves, but are encouraged by our State Department and the United Nations.

I was delighted, one morning to receive an unexpected letter from an old friend whom I had not seen for several years. "I decided," she explained, "to write to someone on every day of Lent." It seemed like a heartwarming idea and a discipline that would bring more joy to others than one might achieve by, for example, abstaining from chocolate. I have since tried the plan myself and find it rewarding in many ways. The letters need not be long. Often they are just notes of congratulation, appreciation, or greeting, but they seem to bring much pleasure. Since it may be difficult to think of forty people, it is helpful to jot down a list ahead of time, adding to it as ideas occur. I like to include in my "Lenten Letters" messages of appreciation to some I do not know personally—an author whose book I like, an editor who has published a fine story or article, a speaker, a radio or television personality, or person in public life whose work I admire.

Recently I enjoyed reading an article along these lines entitled "Be a 4-Cent Philanthropist" by Dwight Wendell Koppes. He described his hobby of writing letters of appreciation to people in all walks of life, including a doctor, a clergyman, a school-board official, a Little League umpire, a streetcar conductor, and an executive. In several cases his letter arrived during a period of discouragement. As a minister expressed it, "Thanks, my friend. Your timing was perfect—you'll never know how perfect!" Koppes' suggestion to those who like the idea but fear they would never actually get started, is to buy some stamps, put them in a dated envelope marked "Bouquets Only," and resolve to write a certain number of letters within a certain time limit.

"Five minutes and a 4-cent stamp and your own special meaning to someone can build a brighter and better life. . . . Be a 4-cent philanthropist." [2]

Long before the days of four-cent stamps an unknown writer of the Old Testament summed up the whole matter in one sentence, a sentence that might well be posted above any writing desk: "As cold waters to a thirsty soul, so is good news from a far country." (Prov. 25:25.)

# 5

## HOW TO HELP THE HANDICAPPED

**THE DEAF**

I remember as a small child an occasion when my grandmother, a very old lady crippled with arthritis, was to have a visit from her sister who lived some distance away. They had not met for several years, and my grandmother looked forward eagerly to the day. When the time came my frail great-aunt was escorted to her sister's room. They embraced—eyes shining with joy at being together—but it turned out to be a sad meeting for they found that they were both so hard of hearing that with their gentle voices they could not make themselves heard. My mother interpreted for them, but that was a poor substitute for direct conversation. Here they were together, but it might have been easier to stay apart and remember each other as the active women of earlier years. Both had accepted growing deafness as part of getting older and had done nothing about it. These were the days before much help was available.

Today, with the onset of impaired hearing, people of all ages are encouraged to have careful medical examination, to equip themselves with the best mechanical aids available and to study the art of lip reading. In my grandmother's day deafness was simply deafness. Now we know there are different types, the two main ones being conduction, which is due to some obstruction, and nerve or perceptive deafness due to loss of nerve fibers or sensory cells. The appropriate hearing aid is determined by the type. Surgery can help in some cases.

The problems involved in deafness are not limited to those of actual hearing. According to Dr. Clarence D. O'Connor, superintendent of the Lexington School for the Deaf in New York City, "Deafness is one of the most crippling of handicaps. Its crippling effects are not of the body, but are of a social, educational, and economic nature." He points out that in early times the deaf were destroyed or hidden way. As recently as 150 years ago, in the early days of our country, it was considered a waste of time to try to teach them. Today in New York and in some other states, it is possible for every deaf child to acquire a complete education and to learn to be self-supporting.

For the child born deaf it is agreed that training should begin in the toddler stage, the earlier the better, to facilitate social adjustment. In many places there are nursery schools and special classes for deaf preschoolers. Where these are not available many families have been helped by the home-study course offered by the John Tracy Clinic, founded by Mrs. Spencer Tracy, in Los Angeles.

Our concern, however, is not primarily deafness, but rather the problems of those who hear, in their understanding of and relationship to the deaf. Hearing aids today are a far cry from the bulky "trumpets" of early invention, but they do not solve all the troubles. A charming friend of mine recently acquired a small hearing aid. When I asked her how she liked it, she said, "It's fine until people notice it. Then they seem to shout! If they would only speak naturally!"

Another friend, with a very deaf member of the family, put her thoughts in these eloquent words: "The hearing aid is magical and factual. It lacks imagination, consideration, and thoughtfulness. These three ingredients of happy daily existence must be furnished by the family."

My friend also tells me that since the very deaf must pick up ideas without all the details, it is often useless to try to tell gossip or anecdotes that depend on inflection or twists of words. Because whispers do not carry on hearing aids, a small pad and pencil come in handy many times, such as at meetings or in church. It is important to discover the best distance and position for conversation. One should remember, too, that the ordinary crashes of a household, such as slamming doors, sound quite different through amplification. Their sudden roar can frighten the deaf person into thinking some disaster has befallen house or family. Avoid these when possible.

The choice of a hearing aid can be confusing and difficult, particularly for older people, who may not realize that there will have to be some experimenting to find the right one and, even then, a period of adjustment before it attains its maximum of usefulness. It is helpful for a friend or relative to become informed on the subject and go along with the deaf person to give encouragement and to aid in making decisions.

New skills in communication were developed after World

War II, when rehabilitation took giant strides. These stressed the importance of learning speech reading, as well as using a suitable hearing aid. The deaf person does not attempt to get every word by either channel, but reaches, rather, for ideas. One teacher, citing a clever, if uneducated speech reader, reported his explanation in these words: "I figures out where you're going, and I beats you there."

According to Greydon G. Boyd, after a hearing loss there are six parts to a complete rehabilitative program, although not all are essential to every case. These are: examination and counseling; medical, perhaps surgical treatment; selection of a hearing aid and auditory training; speech reading; speech correction and improvement; vocational guidance.[1]

In cities throughout the country today there are audiology centers where information and help are available in carrying out such programs.[2] One of the best known is the New York League for the Hard of Hearing which has served as a model for many others.

In communicating with the hard of hearing, associates may take many thoughtful measures. Here are a few:

If a person hears better with one ear than another, notice which is the best side and address him or place him accordingly.

Encourage one who is reluctant to use a hearing aid to make it a practice. It does not set him apart, but, rather, brings him into the circle.

Fill him in on the background of a conversation when he joins a

[1] *Hearing Loss: What Can Be Done about It* (Philadelphia: J. B. Lippincott Company, 1959).

[2] A directory of centers may be obtained from Audiology Foundation, Box 21, Glenview, Ill.

group with such a lead as, "We were just discussing the World Series. Who do you think will win?"

In a group or small meeting seat him near the speaker, but not where bright light will shine in his eyes or deep shadow fall on the speaker's face. These conditions make speech reading difficult.

In ordinary conversation, avoid shouting or speaking with exaggerated articulation. Good articulation in a normal voice is best.

An expressive face and gestures make communication easier than speaking with an impassive expression which gives no clue to mood.

Remove cigarette or pipe from mouth when speaking as they interfere with normal lip movement.

At the end of a sentence or story don't drop your voice. Everyone else laughs or reacts in some way, but to the hard-of-hearing the point is lost, and he is reluctant to ask to have it spelled out.

The person who acquires deafness in maturity enters a lonely world where he may be cut off from the whispered secrets of children, the spring songs of birds, the late summer calls of the locust, the casual banter of his friends. By understanding his problem and remembering these simple suggestions you may give much joy and help.

## THE BLIND

A young lawyer wearing dark glasses and carrying a white cane went into a busy restaurant with a friend. When the waitress came to their table, she asked the friend for his order.

"I'll have ham on rye and coffee."

"And what will *he* have?"

"The same," said the lawyer, rather grimly, and as the girl went off he commented, "I almost told her I wasn't deaf and dumb as well as blind—but it just would have hurt her feelings."

"Does this sort of thing happen often?"

"Too often. I suppose it's because people can't catch our eye and don't know what to do about it—but it isn't only waitresses. Go anywhere with a companion and people assume you need someone to interpret. Ah well. . . ."

"I should have asked for your order first, but half the time I forget you're blind."

"Thanks, pal. Make it all the time."

This experience is one of the most common and most humiliating for those who have lost their sight, but there are others.

In helping a blind person, let him take your right arm, rather than your taking his, when you might cross a street or use stairs. This leaves his right arm free to use a cane or hold things. The motion of your body will be helpful as a guide, a more practical procedure than taking his arm to propel him forward into uncertainty.

In giving directions be sure to say "right" or "left" according to the way he is facing. You can't say vaguely "over this way" or "just over there." It is important to be clear and definite.

When showing a blind person to a chair, merely put his hand on the arm or back. The rest is easy for him.

Never shift furniture around without letting him know the new positions. The reason is obvious, but a sighted person is less apt to realize how very important it is to keep doors either fully open or fully shut. A door that is partly open can be the cause of many bruises.

In a strange place tell him quietly where things are and who is there.

In a restaurant read the menu aloud and, possibly, prices. It is in order to ask if he would like to have his meat cut or the cream and sugar put in his coffee. Sometimes it helps to mention where things are on his plate. In training courses often a clockface design is used. "Potatoes at twelve, meat at six, relish at nine o'clock," for example.

When entering a room where there is a blind person say something to let him know you are there and who you are. Let him know, too, when you are leaving, to spare him the all-too-common embarrassment of discovering he has been talking to an empty chair. In a social group, try to see that he finds friends to talk to, but don't force people on him. He would probably rather roam around and visit than sit in one place.

If he uses a guide dog remember that this is a working dog upon whom the master's safety depends. Petting or feeding the dog may be distracting.

A blind person does not have a sixth sense, as some people suppose, but learns to use other senses, such as touch and hearing, more fully. He can often tell time by his own watch, which has a Braille face, or dial the telephone. He is used to the fact that he is blind and does not mind talking about it, nor does it bother him if you use the word "see." He wants to converse like a completely normal person.

Blind people are proud of their accomplishments and feel humiliated if people move in to help without asking them first. It is always proper to ask quietly if a blind person wishes help. If so, follow his suggestions unobtrusively and then, ignoring his handicap, treat him as the interesting individual he is.

Sighted people often think that seeing-eye dogs and a mastery of Braille are solutions to the problems of the blind. Unfortunately the situation is not so simple. Not all blind people like dogs or would find them acceptable in their residences or the places they frequent. There are expenses in maintaining one of these handsome, highly trained animals, and experience has shown that it takes an active, well person to use a guide dog to good advantage. One of our friends turned down two offers of the gift of a dog because he lacks a sense of direction, preferring, instead, to employ students to take him for walks. Because he participates in community affairs, he accepted a tape recorder instead of the dog and uses it constantly.

The same man has a clever technique for making speeches. Because he would be unable to consult notes, he writes a question on each of about a dozen file cards, numbers them, and distributes them to his audience. The holder of card 1 asks his question, and when this is answered question number 2 is read. This plan has the added advantage of giving the audience a sense of participation.

Learning to read Braille has opened the door of learning and enjoyment for thousands of blind people, but not everyone finds it possible to master the skill. Fingertips may be insensitive or, especially for older peole, the task of learning too great. Fortunately there is a growing supply of fine books and magazines on records and tapes.

Reading material, both in the form of Braille books and recorded talking books, is available free of charge through the Library of Congress in Washington. The American Foundation for the Blind publishes a list of topics mailed every two months to registered readers. Talking book machines are also available without charge for those who are eligible. Full information may be obtained from the Foundation.

Less well known, but greatly appreciated by the Protestant blind, is the work of the John Milton Society, which distributes religious materials both in Braille and on records.[3] A Braille

[3] John Milton Society, 475 Riverside Drive, N. Y., N. Y.

magazine for children is available each month; a religious library is maintained for children, adults, pastors, and teachers. Especially valued are the Sunday-school lessons with teachers' notes, the World Day of Prayer programs, and books of hymns and carols. The Society also provides a pastoral counseling service for those who are isolated and cannot attend church.

Upon receipt of the name of a blind person, the Society will send him the "John Milton Talking Book Magazine," a pair of excellent, long-play records, mailed out four times a year. They contain fine music, talks by outstanding religious leaders, and information of special interest. Unlike the Library of Congress records, these are not to be returned, but to be kept as gifts. Experience shows that they are treasured and usually passed around for others to enjoy. This work is supported by contributions from individuals and groups. The Talking Book Magazine makes a welcome and inspirational gift.

Juliet Bindt's *A Handbook for the Blind* contains valuable information both for the one who has lost his sight and for his family since the author herself is blind and has worked with many others.[4] In *The Lighted Heart* Elizabeth Yates, well known for her stories for young readers, tells how her husband gradually lost his sight. She gives a poignant but inspiring account of the problems and adjustments in a way which not only tells the story of two people, but also offers guidance for others.

In discussing gifts, for instance, she wrote:

Presents for Bill invariably intrigued the imaginations of his friends. There was one who always made him a box of fudge; one liked to send him a tie whose texture was definite and unmistakable;

[4] New York: The Macmillan Company, 1952.

from another came a box of pine soap, fragrant as the woods after rain. And books: the kind that were good for family reading aloud.[5]

Her own gift, on one exciting birthday, was a small piece of shore frontage on a lake not far from their old farmhouse, where he could swim and camp.

Those who face blindness themselves, or for members of their families, will find much help available through the American Foundation for the Blind [6] which serves as a clearing house of information, conducts research, and channels helpful counsel through local agencies. In their leaflet *When You Meet a Blind Person*, which offers personal and practical suggestions, we read:

Today or tomorrow you may meet someone who is blind. When you do, remember that he is an individual with his own distinct personality. . . . He can hear, walk, make decisions. . . . and he is pursuing most of the same daily activities he engaged in as a seeing man.

There are many ways in which you can help a blind person to meet everyday situations. You will find that, in most cases, this means little or no extra effort on your part, except for extending the simple, thoughtful courtesies that you offer any other individual.

## THE DISABLED

The young woman in the wheel chair came to the elevator. When he saw her, another passenger hurried to take hold of the chair and push it aboard. "Thank you," said the young

[5] New York: E. P. Dutton & Company, 1960.

[6] American Foundation for the Blind, Inc., 15 West 16th Street, New York 11, N. Y.

woman politely, but a shadow crossed her face. "Why," she reflected, "don't people let me manage for myself—or at least *ask* if I want help?"

For a patient who has lain helpless for many months, each new achievement is a personal triumph, whether it is turning on a light or opening a door. These are simple enough things for people who do them without thinking, but, when muscles must be trained again, each accomplishment is a step back into the march of living, a step toward the shining goal of independence.

A person who has had no close contact with the handicapped may be sympathetic and eager to help but embarrassed by not knowing what to do. What is the helpful approach?

I took my question to staff members of the beautiful Institute of Physical Medicine and Rehabilitation overlooking the East River in New York City. Here I learned that the most important rule is allowing the patient to do things for himself, even if the struggle is difficult to watch. Nothing is regarded as impossible before a disabled person tries it. If someone has difficulty speaking do not finish his sentences, but listen patiently until the painfully articulated words are completed. Accomplishment builds confidence, and confidence is needed by those handicapped in any way. Be ready to help, but be sure the help is welcome.

I was told that when patients are recovering from crippling illness or accidents there is a psychological period of mourning for the loss of arms, legs, or other faculties. This depression may last for several months, but it is normal and is regarded as a healthy step toward recovery. It is better for the depression to come then than later. Along with this may be a fear of rejection by society.

What should be the attitude of the visitor coming to see a

patient in the depths of suffering and apprehension? There are three possibilities: (1) Come imbued with intense sympathetic sorrow; (2) Look toward future possibilities; (3) Listen. If the caller comes sorrowfully the result is two cases of "Woe is me." This does not help and may deepen the depression. It is more constructive to say, "Yes, I know things look bleak, but there are still a lot of things left you can look forward to. Your accident certainly isn't going to affect your painting or your interest in political affairs."

If the patient indicates that he wants to talk, it is helpful to listen quietly while he unburdens himself of the worries of mental and physical pain. Should he tend to repeat and to go over and over the same ground one may change the course of the conversation by saying gently, "Yes, I understand. You have told me how you feel, but let's look ahead."

The patient should have the opportunity to set the tone of the visit. He may want to pour out his troubles, or he may want to steer away from them. For this reason the tone of the visitor's greeting might well be something neutral, such as "I just stopped in to see how you are getting along," or "How are you feeling?" This leaves the patient free to cue the conversation.

Because friendship and loyalty are so important at times of crisis, letters, cards, and little gifts are strengthening factors. The notes should not dwell on the sadness of the situation, for fear of depressing the patient. His attitude is an important factor in recovery.

Looking beyond the period of hospitalization, I inquired in what ways organizations and communities can better serve their handicapped. Among the suggestions were by offering better educational opportunities and transportation and by more thoughtful building.

More opportunity is needed for handicapped students to pursue higher education. There should be more planning along the lines of the program pioneered by Timothy J. Nugent at the University of Illinois, where he is Director of the Rehabilitation-Education Program. With dormitories adapted for use by both able-bodied and handicapped students the latter can share the campus life. But there is not room for all who apply.

Transportation is a serious problem, except for the fortunate few who can drive their own specially adapted cars. In some communities volunteer organizations transport the handicapped for recreation or medical treatment. Many who work find that taxi fares or costs for special arrangements eat up their slender profits. Any volunteer contribution to this problem is worthwhile.

In planning a new church, school, or public building, the builders should remember those who need ramps, who need space in the aisle for wheel chairs, who need wide doors in telephone booths and rest rooms. It is paradoxical that for so many years churches always seemed to be built at the top of a steep flight of steps, while many of the older people served by the church found these a formidable obstacle.[7]

So important to the handicapped are good features of access that one former patient of the Institute compiled a New York directory of the stores, theaters, boat lines, museums, and restaurants that could be visited with the greatest ease. Such a directory might be useful in other communities.

A friend recovering from severe injury offered some special insights into the experience of the convalescent. "The patient's

[7] Under the auspices of the American Standards Association, Inc., 10 East 40th Street, New York, a study is being made of "Facilities in Public Buildings for Persons with Physical Handicaps."

attitude," she explained, "can be a greater help or handicap than the actual physical condition. When visitors call, especially soon after the injury, it is helpful for them to find out the state of mind of the patient from a relative, someone in the hospital, or the pastor. Coming informed makes possible a much more understanding contact."

When a patient goes home, transportation during the day may present problems—even if the family has a car. If there are church or club meetings that the person would enjoy, the most appreciated gesture is not simply an offer of transportation to the door, but having someone say, "I wonder if you would like to go with me to the meeting on Wednesday? I can stop for you and it would be nice to have you with me." Companionship on the way and during the event means much more than transportation only.

In dealing with the handicapped, it is important to remember that, although the body is impaired, the person is whole, as full of hopes, fears, and aspirations as everyone else. He does not want to be thought of as different. Therefore we should concentrate our attention on his spirit, his interests, and his personality.

Sometimes through adversity and seeming tragedy a life becomes an unexpected channel of service. Who knows what the fruits of suffering may be? On a bronze tablet in the lobby of the Institute on the East River are engraved these lines by an anonymous author:

I asked God for strength that I might achieve,
I was made weak that I might learn humbly to obey,
I asked for health that I might do greater things,
I was given infirmity that I might do better things,

I asked for riches that I might be happy,
I was given poverty that I might be wise,
I asked for power that I might have the praise of man,
I was given weakness that I might feel the need of God,
I asked for all things that I might enjoy life,
I was given life that I might enjoy all things.
I got nothing I asked for, but everything I had hoped for.
Almost despite myself my unspoken prayers were answered.
I am, among all men, most richly blessed.

# 6

## HELPFUL ATTITUDES
## TOWARD ALCOHOLISM

Have you ever started down a long, slippery hill and had the brakes of your car fail to hold? The terrible helplessness of such an experience is something to haunt dreams. In any community we have people around us who have suffered the kindred disaster of alcoholism. Some have fought their way through to renewed control, but many others live in uncertainty. Since some of these lives will touch on ours, it is well to seek an understanding of their problem. To do this we will look first at the national picture, then see it in terms of personal experience, and, finally, consider how nonalcoholics may be helpful.

It is estimated that there are about 70,000,000 people in this country who drink alcoholic beverages at least occasionally, and for perhaps 5,000,000 of these alcohol presents serious problems. The term "alcoholic" does not mean a "down-and-outer" or even a heavy drinker, but refers to the person on any social level who can no longer control his drinking. While the number of alcoholics is estimated at 5,000,000, this is by no means the total of those who suffer through this compulsion. If we multiply this figure by the wives, husbands, children, and parents who undergo the long agony of shame and deprivation we glimpse a truer estimate.

As recently as 1943 no state or city government was doing anything for alcoholics, except throwing them in jail when they became troublesome. To be sure, Alcoholics Anonymous had begun its work on a small scale in the 30's, and a few hospitals, clinics, and doctors were dealing with alcoholics as sick people. The general view, however, was that "drunkards" were disgraceful, irresponsible characters whose moral fiber was too weak to control their appetites. Preaching, punishing, scolding, and appealing to their better natures were the usual and not very successful approaches.

Today the concept resulting from a generation of intensive study is that alcoholism is a form of sickness involving both physical and emotional factors and should be treated as such. Paralleling the fight to bring new public understanding of mental illness has been the crusade to educate people on the basic truths of alcoholism.

The Yale Center of Alcohol Studies carries on scientific inquiries into cause, effect, and methods of treatment. The National Council on Alcoholism, with branches in 58 cities, serving as a clearing house for information, interprets scientific findings into terms the public can understand.[1] Sharing the conviction that this is a public health problem, the World Health Organization of the United Nations has set up an Alcoholism Committee to study the matter along with such ills as malaria and tuberculosis.

Turning from organizations and statistics, let us look at alcoholism through the eyes of Mrs. K, who has found the way back from disaster to normal life. This delightful person, with her husband, a professional man, and her teen-age children, moved a few years ago from another city to a pleasant suburb. The neighbors found them agreeable, although not much interested in "partying." Mrs. K soon became busy with community affairs and had several meetings to attend in the evening. The neighbors did not know that one of the first organizations she joined was the local group of Alcoholics Anonymous. They still did not know it when her husband was transferred five years later. This was the story she told me:

If anyone had predicted I would become an alcoholic, I would have laughed, because, in the beginning, I did not even like the taste of liquor, yet the habit of drinking grew. The more I tried to stop, the more of a nightmare it became. I was one of those people drinking from compulsion. I tried and tried to stop, and my husband did all he could to help, but, after a while, it seemed as if I was living in a fog much of the time. For days I would hardly know what I was doing—and yet I had a wonderful husband, lovely children, all the things people long for. Then, when my mind would clear, I would feel so ashamed I couldn't face it and start looking for escape in the same old way. One night, when things were about

[1] National Council on Alcoholism, 2 East 103rd Street, New York 29, N. Y.

as bad as they could be, my husband came to the table where I was sitting and put a newspaper ad in front of me. It said, "Is alcohol your problem? We can help you. Call. . . ." I knew nothing, beyond the name, about Alcoholics Anonymous, but in that moment something clicked and I felt this might be an answer. I tried to dial the number but was unable even to do that simple thing. My husband completed the call and said his wife was looking for help. Within an hour, a wonderful AA member, who happened to be a woman doctor, appeared at our door. She talked with me for an hour. The next day she took me to her home. I was with her for two days, and then we went to my first group meeting. I was still too foggy to understand everything, but I had the most wonderful feeling of release and peace. I had thought I was alone—the only queer one—the uncontrolled drinker, and here were these fine, wonderful people, and everyone of them had been through it. I knew they could help because they understood.

It wasn't done overnight, Mrs. K explained. When an alcoholic reaches the low point of despair, the process has been going on a long time with damage to both body and emotions. Recovery, as with any other illness, takes time and patience.

Mrs. K told me about the operation of AA in the area of our medium-sized city. There are meetings within driving distance, some in outlying communities, each night of the week. Many of them are held in church social rooms. Most meetings are open to the public and are of special interest to friends and relatives of alcoholics. They have a program of speakers, discussion, and a social period during which coffee and perhaps doughnuts are served. A few meetings are limited to members and reserved for more personal discussion. Members are addressed by their first names and the strictest anonymity is observed at all times outside. She explained the importance of accepting the "Twelve Steps" and outlined some of them:

We had to admit we were powerless over alcohol and that our lives had become unmanageable;

Believe that a Power greater than ourselves can restore us to sanity;

Make a decision to turn our will and our lives over to the care of a God as we understand him;

Make a list of all persons we have harmed and become willing to make amends to all;

Seek through prayer and meditation to improve our conscious contact with God, praying only for knowledge of his will for us and for the power to carry that out;

Having had a spiritual experience as the result of these steps, try to carry this message to other alcoholics and to practice these principles in all our affairs.

What about Mrs. K's previous religious life, which did not seem to help solve her problem? She explained:

I think that my religious experience was rather typical. I went to church, but it seemed that my prayers to control my drinking were not answered. I became cynical, thought church people were hypocritical, and finally felt that there could be no God—especially one who, as we were taught, was kind and just. You see, I wanted God to help me on my own terms. I used to sound off on these doubts when I began going to AA meetings, and then, one day, listening to the experience of another member, I suddenly realized that my prayers were being answered, not in the way I had expected, but through the influence of the wonderful group where we begin by admitting we are powerless alone and then setting out to help others. I attend church regularly now and realize that my hostility was simply guilt expressed in resentment toward others.

Asked if she is beyond temptation today, Mrs. K replied candidly:

No one is ever beyond temptation, but I have lost all desire for drinking. One important point to remember is that the alcoholic *must never again touch liquor*. Experience has proved this, but, because it looks like such a completely impossible prospect, particularly in the beginning, we have worked out a system of facing our problem for one day at a time. . . . No, I don't expect to "graduate" from AA, but, because there is therapy and strength in sharing a problem with others, I expect to continue to attend meetings regularly and be on call whenever I am needed. Are you familiar with the prayer we use? It means so much to so many of us: "God grant me the serenity to accept the things I cannot change, the courage to change the things I can and the wisdom to know the difference."

Mrs. K is one of the wise and fortunate persons who have availed themselves of the help given so generously to those who turn to Alcoholics Anonymous, an organization born of need and compassion. Although its membership, somewhere between 150,000 and 300,000, includes a minority of those in alcoholic trouble, it has restored blighted lives with a high percentage of success.

Because the right attitude on the part of the family is so important and because their problems are so grievous, a new branch known as the Al-Anon Family Groups has grown up. Here relatives may find understanding, fellowship, guidance, and a center of interest paralleling that of the alcoholic, who may suddenly seem to be spending a great deal of his time and enthusiasm on

AA activities. More recently teen-age children of AA and Al-Anon groups have come together in many places to form their own groups, known as Alateen. These young people who have grown up with unhappiness find incentive in their meetings together to understand the problems of their parents and to live useful, responsible lives themselves. All three of the groups, those for alcoholics, those for their families, and those for the young people, stress the study of the Twelve Steps, the use of the "Serenity Prayer," and faith in a God of their understanding.

No specific cause and cure has been found for alcoholism, but increasing evidence shows that there are physical reasons why one person cannot tolerate a drink that would not affect another and emotional reasons which aggravate the compulsion. Therefore, the treatment must include both physical restoration and relief of tensions as well as strengthening the will to recover.

While there is much information available for the alcoholic and his family, there has not, until recently, been more than a suggestion here and there of how friends can be helpful. Fortunately, Mrs. Marty Mann, executive director of the National Council on Alcoholism, has recognized this need in her book *New Primer on Alcoholism*.[2]

From the chapter "What to Do about an Alcoholic," here are some of her suggestions for the nonalcoholic.

Inform yourself through reading and attending open meetings of AA where members give invaluable insight into their problems and the things that help.

Recognize as a myth the idea that the ability to drink a great deal is a sign of prowess. This primitive conception can be very dangerous as it implies that nondrinkers are weaklings.

[2] New York: Holt, Rinehart & Winston Company, 1958.

Recognize, too, as a myth the tradition that alcoholic drinks mean hospitality. There are better forms than pressing a glass on someone who has declined it. That one drink may destroy a hard won resistance.

At the other extreme, never harp on the alcoholic's condition by, for example, passing one sort of drink to others and leaving a conspicuous glass of tomato juice on the tray which is passed to him last! The choice and decision must be his.

Lectures, preaching and nagging usually increase guilt with escape in the same old pattern.

Mrs. Mann believes that friends can get across important information and arouse interest in a constructive program of action, which means looking for help. Sometimes it is possible to arrange a meeting between an alcoholic friend and one who has recovered, or an AA member. The important thing to remember is that the sooner he seeks help from a qualified person he can trust, whether doctor, clergyman, social worker, psychologist, or counselor, the better his chances for recovery.

In the growing concern of industry for rehabilitating the alcoholic, emphasis is put on the idea that covering up for a fellow employee is a lesser kindness than helping him to get early treatment. This has salvaged many careers.

All authorities agree that more research, more public education, and better use of the wisdom we now have are needed. In a moving personal experience article, "I Am the Widow of an Alcoholic," Virginia Conroy stressed her regret that she did not inform herself more fully about the nature of alcoholism during her husband's troubled life. She offered this thought in conclusion:

If you want to help in the fight on alcoholism and assets are limited, you can do it simply by changing your vocabulary. Every time you hear a person spoken of as a drunkard, correct that statement. Say, "No, he is not a drunkard. He is an alcoholic and he is ill. He needs treatment. What treatment is available in his community? What can be done about it?" [3]

[3] Reprinted from *Today's Health*, published by the American Medical Association.

# 7

## HELPFUL ATTITUDES
## TOWARD MENTAL ILLNESS

When a friend, a neighbor, or a business associate has suffered mental illness what are the ways to be helpful? After a patient has left the mental hospital, many people are baffled as to what to say or what not to say. They are embarrassed and perhaps try to avoid him for this reason. This is unfortunate because a fear that haunts the minds of many former mental patients is the fear of nonacceptance. If he feels that people reject him it shakes his none-too-rugged self-confidence.

John Jones, for example, after being so emotionally distraught that many people knew of his condition, went to a mental institution where he received modern drug and shock treatments with psychotherapy. After only a few weeks his condition had improved so greatly that he was allowed to come home.

The first day he walked down the street of his home town to his office he thought people looked at him with surprise and curiosity. One woman acquaintance, he was sure, scurried off in the opposite direction. A man said, with embarrassment, "Hello, John. Looks like rain, doesn't it? I've got to be getting along." But, a few minutes later, a friend came over and held out his hand, "We know you've been in the hospital, John. Missed seeing you around. I sure hope you're feeling better."

"Thanks," said John, "I appreciate that. I'm getting back into the swing of things now."

"Good. My wife and I were saying we'd like to drop over some evening."

John went on his way, standing a little straighter and with more courage in his heart.

The experience of being committed to a mental hospital can be one of life's most difficult ordeals, both for the troubled patient and for his family. It is heartbreaking to see a beloved person reduced to behavior that is a mockery of a fine personality. In other ages the label would have been "possessed of a devil," or at a later time "hopelessly insane." Today, fortunately, it is "mental illness," and there are some spectacularly effective new treatments.

What is mental illness? It is not a single disorder, such as appendicitis, but corresponds to the term "physical illness" in that it covers conditions ranging from actual physical damage to the brain to emotional disturbances that become troublesome under stress. There are three major types of mental disorders. (1) The psychoses require hospitalization and are characterized by severe mood disturbances and withdrawal from reality. (2) The neuroses are less severe emotional disturbances, anxieties, and tensions, which may be treated in doctor's office or clinic while the patient continues to go to work. (3) Personality disorders are difficulties in adjustment finding outlet in such behavior as that of the alcoholic, the drug addict, the delinquent, and the chronic gambler, or are translated into physical ailments.

Everyone knows of relatives or friends with such personality patterns. Psychiatrists know how to decide which type or types of disorder are characteristic of a person and can determine the best treatment, if this is needed. Each and every one of us has problems which we control and handle as best we can. In the words of one social worker, "Exposure to someone who has lost control 'hits home,' and we may feel either superior or sympathetic, thinking 'there, but for the grace of God, go I.'"

Many people do not realize this new depth of understanding. To them anyone with mental illnes is "crazy" and possibly dangerous. Cutting remarks come back to the ex-patient, and naturally they hurt, but they fall into perspective if a relative or friend can say, "Some people have a lot to learn—just the way we did."

It is important, too, for children to understand, both the children in the family and those with whom they associate. The roots of most mental disturbances go back to childhood and often children understand an unhappy adult better than other grown-ups. Unfortunately, children may be influenced by the attitudes of their parents and may toss out such comments as "Your father's crazy and had to go to the nuthouse"—much as they would say "My father can beat up your father."

This is a bitter taunt for a child, already disturbed by strange upheavals in his home life. If he has had the situation explained to him and is assured of continuing love in his family he can stand his ground and reply, "My father isn't crazy. He was

70

sick and had to go to the mental hospital. Now he's better and going back to work next week."

While the patient is hospitalized there is opportunity to give comfort and companionship to his family. There may be a need, too, for legal aid or financial help. Those at home are experiencing a special sort of loneliness. It is painful to see a beloved character seem to disintegrate, and with this change the whole foundation of emotional life is shaken. Here is loneliness, not only because of the physical absence of the patient, but loneliness for his truly loved self. The visits to the hospital are apt to be difficult and taxing. If there are children at home there is an extra burden of responsibility, extra strains and tensions. It is during these weeks that true friends can do much to help —offering transportation for hospital visits, care and good times for the children, companionship during lonesome evenings, and the many thoughtful remembrances, whether hot casseroles or new books, that in little ways will help.

During these troubled days an understanding pastor can be of great assistance. Large mental hospitals usually have specially trained resident chaplains, Catholic, Jewish, and Protestant. These men, working in harmony with the doctors, can give special strength to both patient and family. The patient's own pastor is free to visit and, according to the social-service supervisor of a large institution, can be of great help—if he, too, works in co-operation with the doctors.

Because counseling is becoming so important a part of religious ministry, today's seminary students have increasing opportunity to learn the relationships of mental and spiritual health. Many churches offer counseling services. Frequently an individual who is distraught would rather talk over his problems in a pastor's study than brave the unknown precincts of psychiatry. If, in his opinion, the troubled one needs further and more intensive treatment, the pastor can explain the reason and procedure in a reassuring fashion that makes the step seem desirable. Family service societies also stand ready to help.

When a mother needs extended hospital care, foster home agencies may be able to arrange for children to live with a family where the father can keep in touch until the mother can again carry home responsibilities. Some communities have homemaker services, with trained women who substitute for the mother and make it possible for the children to stay in familiar surroundings.

Often the patient does not come home to stay, as he would following an operation. He may be allowed to come for a day, a day and a night, a weekend, or whatever the doctor feels wise. To most patients home looks like the promised land after hospitalization, but the transition from the routine and attention of a well-run hospital to the upsets and commotions of a lively family is not always easy. As with a child after an illness, when the mental patient finds he is no longer the center of attention, he may not be his most agreeable self. Furthermore, the family must face the possibility that he may have to return to the hospital. Sometimes after patients return home they spend their days at special centers for further treatment until the adjustment is more nearly made.

The patient comes home with a new understanding of his problems resulting from the psychotherapy or counseling sessions with his doctor, but he may be apprehensive, not only about acceptance by others, but about future employment. Back on the job, whether as homemaker or employee, the chances are that, like an athlete out of training, he will not at first be able to work at capacity. With patience and understanding on the part of associates, however, he will gradually regain former abilities.

To help him fit back into his accustomed niche, both socially and in the office, it is helpful to bring him up to date on the things that have been happening in order that he may not suddenly run into embarrassing gaps of information. He may be apprehensive of meeting old associates, and usually small groups are better than large parties, which may tax him with too much excitement.

Mental patients returning to loving families and former jobs have adjustments to make and problems to master, but much worse are the cases of those isolated persons who have no waiting welcome. For them the silence of a rented room is more ominous than the humming routines of a hospital, with cheerful nurses and interested doctors. In some states there is provision for family care, a system resembling that of foster homes for children. This makes possible placement of convalescent cases in carefully chosen families when patients would do better away from former surroundings, when relatives are hostile, or when there are no relatives. In some places residences known as "halfway houses" are most helpful as temporary homes.

There are many forlorn persons who, upon release, experience a terrible and destructive loneliness. Fountain House in New York City represents a pioneer effort to meet this problem by serving as a hospitable day center for former mental patients of many races and backgrounds.[1] There are almost six hundred members who drop in or spend the day. The program, carried out by a trained staff assisted by volunteers, offers hobby groups, employment training, and companionship. Its long range pur-

[1] 412 West 47th Street—former mansion of Alexander Woollcott.

pose is to reduce the number of those who relapse and must go back to hospitals by offering professional help in an atmosphere of warm and meaningful contacts with people. A staff member, asked what in her opinion was the greatest need in this type of work, told me:

We need volunteers to come in and help with the program. Some may have special skills and be able to teach classes, but the important thing is that volunteers form a link with the real world outside. If the patient behaves in an unusual fashion he can see the effect on a normal person, and this is helpful. There are many opportunities for volunteers across the country, and working with mental patients is a tremendously valuable service.

What, then, are the helpful attitudes toward mental illness? You may help by learning through reading something of the nature of the problem; standing by the family of the hospitalized patient; and when he returns, by showing faith in his recovery by helping him fit back into his job, recreation, and community life. In organizations it is helpful to assign him a small job, which shows he belongs, but not one that would be burdensome. To help on a wider scale a person with a special concern can volunteer to work in a local institution and also can campaign for better public education and clinical facilities.

Most important, by learning more about the problems of mental health we can inform and influence others to look upon mental illness as something that can be diagnosed and treated. We can help people realize that one of the miracles of modern medicine is the progress made in one generation toward bringing so many of the mentally ill out of the darkness and back into the sunshine of everyday life.

# 8

## HOW TO HELP THE AGING

Mrs. Evans, white haired and a bit stiff from arthritis, sat down on the park bench to rest. A little girl, yellow curls bobbing as she skipped rope, gave her a friendly smile when she stopped for breath.

"You skip very well," Mrs. Evans told her. "How old are you?"

"Going on six. How old are you?"

"How old would you guess?"

"A hundred."

"Not quite," Mrs. Evans smiled ruefully. "Do you know that once I had hair like yours and liked to skip rope?"

The child looked at her with no comprehension of such an unlikely fact and, wisely, changed the subject. "I have a kitten," she announced and skipped off.

"That's the real trouble," Mrs. Evans reflected watching the sunlit child. "People can't believe I am the same person I always was inside—that it's just the appearance that changes."

In helping older people the basic need is to remember that whatever the physical changes the essential person has not changed in the basic human need for affection and recognition.

The problems of any group of older persons are apt to be loneliness, physical impairment, poverty, lack of purposeful activity. Because each of these is multiplied by so many individuals, these are problems on a large scale. Our elder citizens, because of longer life expectancy, are becoming a larger segment of our population—at a time when houses are smaller and when many of the homemaking operations have been simplified, eliminating the little tasks once assumed by grandmothers and aunties. No longer do lamp chimneys need polishing, and where, in these days of orlon, is the heaping basket of socks waiting for skilled fingers to darn their holes ?

It might be pointed out, however, that no inventor has yet succeeded in mechanizing the processes of infant care. With the revival of large families many a home is enriched beyond measure by the loving assistance of a grandmother. It should be established, too, that grandmothers have changed, as well as houses and housekeeping. Their world is no longer only domestic, but often career or community centered.

This discussion, however, is focused on the later years, when activities are more limited and many beloved companions have gone. This is a part of life that calls urgently for understanding. To take our thinking of the realms of theory and statistics, we will present a variety of situations in human terms.

Loneliness is a weary ache of the heart. Mrs. Jones, who had lost her husband, sisters, and many old friends, finally was persuaded to come East from California and live with her married daughter in a suburb. The location was pleasant, but church and stores were beyond walking distance. There was not much for Mrs. Jones to do, and she had no contact with contemporaries and no old associations. Her daughter's friends were pleasant, but they moved in a different world. The teen-age grandchildren moved in their own world too. Although living in attractive surroundings, Mrs. Jones found life a forlorn thing and sometimes felt as if she were stranded on an island in a busy highway with traffic charging past on both sides. It saddened her to realize that it would be simpler for all concerned if she were not in her daughter's house.

Mrs. Jones' situation looked ideal to Mr. Tuttle, who rented a room, cooked for himself, and had no family. He didn't bother to shave or put on a clean shirt very often. He was resigned but wished there were someone who cared what happened to him.

Miss Allen saved frugally during the years she was working as a cook but had to give up when her strength failed. Her savings did not go very far. She did not have social security and shrank from the idea of "going on welfare." She didn't eat much, couldn't afford new clothes or carfare—and woke up in the night afraid.

Mr. Beggs thought retirement was going to resemble life in the promised land, but when he had had his fill of fishing and had the roof mended and the painting done his thoughts kept turning back to the office, and he was as restless as a bear in a cage. This did not make life any easier for Mrs. Beggs, who was accustomed to seeing her friends and going her own way from nine to five. Now she had a rather edgy man around the house at all hours. No one thought he was important any more, and he didn't like it.

These are unhappy stories, but each is true of many people. A member of the Society of Friends once summed up the matter with quiet eloquence by saying that what the aging want is "somewhere to live, something to do, and someone to care." To this we might add "and something to live on."

Those who associate with poorly adjusted elders have their special problems. Mary Miller and her mother were never truly congenial, but financial straits necessitated doubling up. The mother was critical to the point where the grandchildren avoided her and stayed away from home for their social life. Her feelings were hurt when she was not included in social activities, but she made no effort to find friends and interests of her own. The home was full of tensions, and Mary was torn by conflicting loyalties.

Tom White, a kindly soul, whose father-in-law lived with the family, was always courteous, but the repetition of long stories about people he never knew almost drove him to drink.

Is there any help for such situations? In many cases, yes, through constructive action based on understanding. Before discussing solutions, however, let us digress to recognize that, if aging presents heartaches, it can also be marked by gallantry and lived with generosity.

Most of us can think of two people of similar age, background, and resources whose lives are quite different. Mrs. A lives alone, has few interests, finds much to criticize, and likes to discuss her ailments. She has few visitors and leads an emotionally drab existence. Mrs. B has more serious ailments, but loves people and laughter. She likes to make new friends, welcomes the neighborhood children, has a telephone that rings often, keeps the kettle ready for a friendly cup of tea, likes to read, and keeps up with the world through books and television. In spite of its shadows she finds life good.

In Prov. 23:7 we read that "as [a man] thinketh in his heart, so is he," and it seems that the way he is can determine the climate of his life. Character cannot control the disasters and sorrows that may befall any of us, but there are different ways of meeting the same troubles and different capacities for recognizing the good and lovely things of life.

John Hunter, a retired engineer, had a long-time hobby of workshop tinkering. When he and his wife bought a little home in a new development the neighbors soon learned how handy he was with his tools, but after many services were reluctant to ask further favors. "All right," John told his wife when he realized this. "I'll make it a business." With a modest scale of prices John now has a busy time helping out his neighbors for a price he considers fair and which they consider a great bargain since he is always available and interested.

Mrs. Burroughs, an attractive woman of advanced years, lived alone in an adobe studio in a Southwestern community. An Indian girl came in to clean and help in the kitchen when she had guests, which was often. The home was small and unpretentious, but many books and paintings spoke of a full and cosmopolitan life. Yet Mrs. Burroughs, a widow with no family, came to town a few years earlier knowing no one but thinking it would be a pleasant place to live. By doing volunteer work in the hospital and by joining hobby groups she found a growing circle of friends whom she continued to enjoy, even in less active years.

"What a charming home you have created," I said to her as we visited.

"Thank you," she replied with a little smile. "I believe that a woman should have a setting for the last act."

I know two retired farmers who find pleasure in doing fine work with their gnarled hands as they listen to radio on winter evenings. One has completed a set of needlepoint covers for the dining room chairs. The other, who weaves linen mats on his loom and makes beautiful rugs, enjoys donating choice items to the annual church bazaar.

Even as strength declines it is possible for one of generous spirit to send visitors away enriched.

Mrs. Carter was confined to a charity ward in a hospital. The future held no hope of recovery, yet she found something to give. She liked to keep a jigsaw or crossword puzzle under way, and when people stopped to speak she would ask their help in finding a piece or a word. There was shared pleasure in this tiny pursuit and a sense of accomplishment when the clue was found. Visitors never had to worry about the right thing to say because she, in her gracious understanding, provided a channel of communication.

"My mother-in-law is a joy," a friend told me. "She can't get around now, but her mind is so busy she has no time to feel sorry for herself. She likes to memorize a few lines from Shakespeare or the Bible during the day and then say them over if she wakes up in the night."

Mrs. Bliss, well over eighty, was bedfast and often in pain, but when callers came she took their hands warmly, looked into their eyes with a smile of pleasure, and said, "How are you? Tell me what you have been doing and all about those wonderful children."

People loved her and came often. At her funeral the pastor recounted his first meeting with her. When he came to the local church he found her name on the list of shut-ins and went to call. It was a delightful visit, for he found a bright spirit seasoned with wisdom. When he suggested a prayer before he left, as was his custom, Mrs. Bliss smiled. "Thank you . . . let me pray for *you!*"

Selfless living reaps a harvest in old age, both in love and in the beautiful faces of those who have lived with radiance.

State Senator Thomas E. Desmond of New York, an authority in the field, has said that learning is senility's greatest foe. "Without education of some type the spirit perishes long before the heart stops its beat." [1]

Learning faculties may be rusty from disuse, but may be reactivated, as studies have shown. Education need not be the study of such subjects as economics and physics, but may include any new interest in books, crafts, or group activities.

In many communities golden age or senior citizen groups flourish under the auspices of social agency, adult education, or church. In many other places they are needed to offer an interesting weekly program, an opportunity to visit over refreshments, or a day center where there is always a welcome. While these clubs may not appeal to those fortunate persons rich in family, friends, and interests, there are many others who find here a sparkle of enjoyment they had thought was lost forever. Particularly for the solitary, or as one gifted director has phrased it "for the elderly persons who have allowed themselves to lose contact with the useful stream of society," these clubs offer new horizons of interest and pleasure.

A neighbor could do a great service to the solitary Mr. Tuttle

[1] Mr. Desmond has served as Chairman of the New York State Joint Legislative Committee on Problems of the Aging.

or the forlorn Miss Allen by introducing them to a golden age club. Here they would find companionship, and Miss Allen, by telling her worries to the sympathetic director, could be guided to a social worker who would explain her best course for obtaining financial assistance.

It is sad that so many of those confronted with the problems of aging, either their own or problems of those close to them, do not realize how much helpful wisdom has been distilled from the experience of others and that this wisdom is available for their guidance.

If Mr. Beggs, the restless retiree we met earlier, were to happen on a tiny booklet *Retire and Be Rich*,[2] by Thomas Collins, writer of the syndicated column "Golden Years," he would find in its wise pages an illuminating description of himself and what to do about it.

We met, too, Mary Miller and her difficult mother, whose presence was a disturbing element in her daughter's household. A friend suggested that Mary read *When Parents Grow Old*, by Elizabeth Ogg. In this interesting study she found these paragraphs:

Remember that we are not endowed with the same solicitude for an aging parent as we feel for a child. Caring for the old is a socially implanted responsibility. Our feelings toward our parents are a compound of love and resentment—love for their care and resentment for all the occasions in our childhood when they curbed and punished us. However affectionate our adult relations with them, the underlying resentments are apt to linger. Parents, too, resent as well as love their children.

[2] Golden Years Booklet, Box 1672 Grand Central Station, New York 17, N. Y.

Since we all harbor some such resentments, on one side or the other, we need not feel guilty about them.[3]

The unhappy daughter, torn by conflicting loyalties, found a great light shed on her troubles in this pamphlet, which goes on to discuss creative ideas dealing with living and housing. Sometimes it is more satisfactory an older person to live in a church home or pleasant foster home than with relatives, but the experts stress that we should plan *with* rather than *for* the aging and help them stay in their accustomed homes as long as they wish and it is in any way possible.

One of the best ways of getting away from the long stories of the good old days, really a pathetic sign of lost importance, is to make the present more interesting. It is invaluable to help an older person establish congenial contacts by making it possible for him to attend church, senior citizens or interest groups, to follow up new friendships with home hospitality, or to arrange, by offering transportation, for visits with old friends.

One who has had extensive experience in dealing with older people suggests her own kindly way of dealing with lengthy reminiscences.

Often when a subject comes up, we can tell just which story it will suggest, a story we know by heart and there isn't always time to hear it through. Suppose it is Uncle Jeff's story about a hard-fought election of fifty years ago. Before he is well launched I pick up a word—Democrat, for instance and ask, "Uncle Jeff, how do you think the Democrats are making out this year?" While I feel a little remorse for depriving him of the pleasure of telling his story,

[3] Public Affairs Pamphlet 208, p. 10. Copyright 1957 by the Public Affairs Committee, Inc. Used by permission.

I find that this way it is possible to bypass the story, but not reject the person.

Since each human being hungers for a feeling of worth, it is constructive to find outlets for the skills of the elderly, whether as pie makers, needlewomen, garden experts, or local historians. Earlier hobbies can be resumed, while adult education or other groups offer a variety of new interests.

In dealing helpfully with the aging it is important to try to understand both the problems and the psychology, whether through reading or sympathetic intuition; to co-operate with community and church planning; and to show in many ways of thoughtfulness that there are those who care.

# 9

## HOW TO HELP
## WITH HEARTACHES

When heartaches come to our friends, how can we help? We are not speaking now of the death of those who have lived a full life, poignant though these losses may be, but of the hard-to-explain misfortunes for which there seems to be scant comfort.

A child tumbles off a chair and runs crying to her mother to have a painful bump kissed. While the kiss has not the slightest physical effect on the injury it removes the sense of outrage and the child, ignoring the ache, returns to her game. It is beyond our powers to cure most of the hurts that come to our friends, but we may, through understanding, help remove the sense of outrage and encourage the unhappy ones to re-enter the stream of healing activity.

Heartaches, tragedies, and failures come in infinite variety, but to simplify their discussion, we will consider them under three headings.

1. Personal failure in work, behavior, or relations with others. This group, for which the individual is to some degree responsible, might include job failure, discord, negligence resulting in harm to others, overindulgence, lawbreaking, and marital difficulty. When trouble engulfs a person as a result his heart's cry will be *"What did I do that was wrong?"* or *"How could I have done what I did?"*

2. The heartaches of a loved one. Sometimes the troubles or pain of a child, husband, or wife are more difficult to bear than one's own. Here we have the suffering of the parent for a child crippled by polio or accident, a daughter or son who makes a serious mistake, the burden of a wife whose husband fails in business, the trials of a husband whose wife becomes an alcoholic. Because of close ties of love the anguished question here is *"Could I have helped prevent this?"*

3. Misfortunes completely beyond our control. These might include freak accidents, criminal attacks, disfiguring illness, a mentally retarded child, suffering through such natural forces as hurricanes, tragedies, or war. For unforeseen disasters there arises an age-old question, *"Why does this happen to me?"*

The classic account of man's struggle with misfortune is found in the book of Job, where Job is tested by successive afflictions to prove that a good man exists who would not, in the end, curse God for his sufferings. The book poses timeless questions and ends in affirmation, but the answers are not clear. For example, the modern reader finds it difficult to accept the dreadful deaths of Job's ten innocent children as a test of faith, with the restitution at the end of letting Job have ten more children! Archibald MacLeish, in his moving play *J.B.*, tinkers with the resolution of Job's problem, but not conclusively.

A modern classic dealing with all types of heartache is Alan Paton's *Cry, the Beloved Country*,[1] a story of South Africa distinguished not only for its beautiful, almost biblical language, but also for its Christian insight into the ancient questions. It tells how Kumalo, a simple and devout pastor, leaves his village for the city of Johannesburg to seek a lost sister, a lost brother, and a lost son. It proves to be a trail of bitter sorrows. Why should these agonizing sorrows come to him? Kumalo does not know the answer, but decides to waste no time and strength in brooding about it. "That is a secret," he concludes and puts it from his mind, realizing that tragedy does come to innocent victims and the problem is not to learn why, but to learn how to face it. He is comforted in one dark hour, by an old priest who tells him, "When the storm threatens, a man is afraid for his house, but when the house is destroyed there is something to do. About a storm he can do nothing, but he can rebuild a house."

Kumalo endures his troubles with humility, learns new values, finds that unexpected good can come out of sorrow, and turns a pilgrim's progress of grief into a triumphant story of Christian faith.

1. The simplest to understand, of the three categories of heartache, is that of the person who has, to some degree brought the trouble on himself. For example the student who fails because he did not study, the employee discharged for dishonesty or incompetence, a performer who fails before an audience.

[1] New York: Charles Scribner's Sons, 1948.

87

These are painful experiences, but the time of humiliation is the time for friends to stand by and show their faith in both the individual and his future. A helpful attitude can be "I'm sorry for your trouble but this isn't the end. I know you can work things out." Often it helps to tell of similar experiences, not to "top" the trouble in question, but to show how another overcame difficulties. A candidate is elected after defeats. A student who flunked out of college works a year and returns to his studies with fresh interest and motivation. A young employee who thinks he "knows it all" is told that, for his sake, he should seek more congenial employment. He is indignant, but meeting his former employer a few years later, he greets him in friendly fashion, tells how he himself is now faced with handling cocky young graduates, and adds, "That jolt you handed me was the best thing that ever happened."

Where other people are involved, the blame is more difficult to fix. A marriage breaks up. Whose fault is it? Each blames the other, as marriage counsel records show. This is a natural form of face saving, but it is only when the individual recognizes his own error that the healing process can begin. Sometimes this is impossible and the next step may be divorce. It may bring welcome release but is often painful. One friend described her feelings this way:

It is hard for others to realize the sense of humiliation and failure that goes with a divorce. Our whole structure of living is overturned. There is a terrible rootlessness. Where do I go? What do I do now? You soon learn who really cares about you and who was interested in your social position. Advice, both spoken and written, sometimes in critical vein, comes in large quantities—as though a person could come to this action without thinking of what it entailed. And in your own heart, even after the mind has made its decision, there lingers the painful, unanswerable question, could I have prevented this?

What can people do to help? If they only knew. . . . We want desperately a vote of confidence. They can realize that we are lonely and keep in touch. Sometimes people don't know what to say when they meet an acquaintance after a divorce, whether to mention it or not. I had some letters from people, and other notes on Christmas cards, immediately after it happened, saying they were sorry for the unhappiness. Then when we met face to face there was no awkwardness. I appreciated these messages very much. Usually it is better for the person who has had trouble to decide whether or not to discuss it, but the main thing is this—show you believe in us!

Sometimes there are situations that involve tragic, irrevocable loss. A woman driving on an icy day saw a child with a sled, tried to avoid him, skidded, and killed the little boy. She loved children, and although not held guilty, she could not wipe out the nightmare, even with sleeping pills or alcohol. She brooded and was swept with anguished moments when she cried out, "I just can't stand it." A friend, realizing that human comfort was ineffectual, urged her to talk with an understanding pastor. She went to his study, poured out her story.

"You have an agonizing burden," he agreed, "but you did all you could at the time to avoid the accident. You have made such restitution as is possible, and now you must set your house in order and become a useful person again. You must recognize that we do not know why such tragedies can happen, but, when a burden is so great, you can leave it with God."

And so she found peace as she learned to pray:

Help me to realize that this grief came through no intent of mine and in spite of my effort to prevent it. Bring comfort to the family that mourns and the knowledge that I mourn with them. Help me, Father, to leave this burden at Thy feet and, freed from its weight, to return to useful living in Thy service.

2. What can friends do to help one who is suffering for another? It is important to realize that the mother whose child is stricken with polio or the wife whose husband's career is blighted by his own mistake or another's must stand a little apart from the tragedy to give strength. A woman hears a cry and sees a swimmer foundering. If she jumps in the chances are that she, too, will be dragged under. Instead she runs for a pole and holds it out for the swimmer to grasp. Just so, it is important not to be sucked down in sympathetic suffering, but to remain, seemingly undismayed, on solid ground. In this way one can say, perhaps without words, "I have faith in you and in the future. We can handle this thing." To strengthen one in this attitude is the opportunity and obligation of friends—but not everyone realizes.

A friend, whose child was crippled in an accident, told about the letters she received at the time.

So many were gloomy, full of things like "what a terrible tragedy" or "I don't see how you can stand it." I felt sad enough already and such comments didn't help . . . and we realize increasingly how important it is for all of us to avoid self pity. What did help was a familiar bit of homespun philosophy: "when one door is closed, another will open." This I believe with my whole heart and it is an unfailing source of comfort.

For some perverse reason people are apt to tell the burdened friend about similar and worse cases with sad endings. The sufferer's own problem looms too big at this point for him to be interested in others—unless, as mentioned earlier, these experiences carry a message of hope.

I shall always remember a woman whose husband was undergoing a long ordeal to save his sight. I talked with her one day on the telephone, and her voice was so cheerful that I exclaimed, "You sound in wonderful spirits!"

"I am," she told me. "We've had years when everything went along smoothly, and we just took our religion for granted. Now we have a crisis, and if our faith means anything I figure this is a time of testing."

3. Long before the time of Job, and ever since, disaster has befallen the innocent and unsuspecting. I saw a crowd one day in New York and heard the sirens of an ambulance. A weight used to keep a screen in place had fallen from an apartment window and knocked a man unconscious. He had just come from a birthday luncheon, and within hours he was dead. Why? Who can say? "That is a secret."

A Moslem might say "It is the will of Allah," but if we tried to comfort a stricken friend by saying it is the will of our loving Father the reaction would probably be resentful and hostile. How then, can we offer comfort to a person suffering from forces beyond his control?

During the Korean conflict, friends of ours were notified that their son, an air force pilot, was reported missing behind enemy lines and presumed dead. Through roundabout rumors they suspected there was a chance that he had survived, but it was a thin wisp of hope. The mother described their ordeal in this way:

It was several months before my soul knew any peace, and this came about gradually as I prayed. At first I cried out "Let it not be so" and rebelled that this tragedy had happened to us. It was when I could honestly pray, "Thy will be done" that I found all was well. Had our son been killed, then he would be with God. In reaching out to God for help in great need, there comes a closeness and communion that is very real. We must erase from our hearts all resentment at our fate and trust in him.

After two years the word came suddenly that the son had been released and would soon be home. She said further, "We know we have been blessed, and we understand the suffering of those whose loved ones did not return. I hope that I shall never forget to be thankful, not only to God, but to our many friends who prayed for us."

A heartache which comes to many parents is the retarded child. Ruthie had pretty yellow curls and a sweet smile, but she was not like the other six-year-olds on the block. One day soon after her family had moved in, she was standing with a group of children partway down the block. A mother came out, grasped her own child, and said to Ruthie, "Look. . . . You're not to play here. You go home!"

Ruthie went in distress, not knowing what was wrong. Her mother knew, and it was a familiar pain. Her child was happy and innocent, but the neighbor was afraid of what she did not understand. It would take time to fit in here, but it was encouraging that the children, after their first curiosity, had let Ruthie play at her own pace on the edge of their games.

Sometimes an institution is the best or the only answer. However, through the efforts of the National Association for Retarded Children, special classes are now available in many communities for the severely retarded. Here, under skilled teachers, the children are studied carefully and given the chance to realize their potentialities, however limited. Even if Ruthie can never read more than a few words, she may learn to care for her own needs, to dress neatly, to behave pleasantly, to take directions, to carry out simple tasks, and to finish the things she starts.

One of the things that hurts parents is when acquaintances ignore the existence of such a child. As one mother observed, "Nobody will ever know how much it hurt when I didn't hear from anyone in my church group after my baby was born. They knew something was wrong—and stayed away. Later, if I'd meet them on the street, they would avoid looking at my boy and not even answer when he said 'hello.' It's been ten years now."

In the words of another: "I can't understand it when people send Christmas cards and presents to the rest of us and leave Bobby out. Bobby *is part of our family.*"

This, perhaps, is the heart of the matter for those who seek the helpful aproach to parents whose child is different. Bobby *is* part of the family and is as precious as every other member. No matter how grave his handicaps, he is not a thing, but an individual. Ask about him, remember him, smile at him, speak to him. Show his parents your interest in his progress.

Heartaches may come in many forms—crippling illness, loss of love, betrayal, demotion, disillusion, accident, disaster, personal failure. What can we do to help? We can let our troubled friends know that we are standing by and praying for them. We can listen when it is helpful for them to talk and encourage them to face reality and plan for the future. We can show unshaken faith in the individual despite failure, mistake, and humiliation. We may guide them to others whose wisdom will be of special help. We can suggest laying the burden of grief at the feet of God.

To see a heartache in perspective call up the memory of a vast, panoramic view of the world from a plane or a high mountain. A storm cloud towers up, blots out the sun, and blackens the earth. But this darkness is not the end. After a while it begins to lift and the outlines of farms, pastures, towns, and woodland become clear again in the sunlight, with only portions darkened by the drifting clouds. A tragedy is not the whole, but only a shadowed part of life.

# 10

## HOW TO HELP FIGHT PREJUDICE

A Jewish friend told me a wistful little story about her daughter who was attending kindergarten. The child came home one day in great excitement. "Mommy, all the children are going to have Christmas trees with lights on them. How soon can we get ours?"

My friend looked at the eager face and took a deep breath. A time had come for explanations. She sat down and took her daughter on her lap. "We have our own special celebrations in Jewish families," she began. "Christmas trees are mostly for little Christian children."

Disappointment shadowed the big brown eyes, but after a thoughtful moment the little girl asked hopefully, "But can little Jewish children have snow?"

She was beginning to sense invisible barriers but did not understand what or why. The disappointment would be keener as she understood more. In spite of a wealth of family love and a proud religious heritage it is never easy to find a road blocked off, as it was in the case of a high-school senior. She had worked hard and made an excellent all-around school record to submit to the college of her choice. She was not accepted, but a classmate with a lower record, but of non-Jewish name, was welcomed.

Nor, in maturity, is it easy for the businessman to be barred from a decision-making luncheon at a country club where guests ineligible for membership may not be invited.

In a Northern city the YWCA engaged as director of its Y-Teen program a charming young Negro, whom we will call Betty B. Well groomed, with an excellent education and a good sense of fun combined with skill in group work, she planned the activities for about three hundred girls of mixed races. The girls liked her, the program flourished, but Betty B. was not happy. There was the problem of housing. The best room she could locate in the city of 100,000 was not very attractive and was located in a part of the city where she was afraid to walk past the taverns when she came home after dark. Furthermore, in spite of her activity-filled days, she was lonely. Because of the housing bias, educated Negroes who considered working in the area, usually moved elsewhere. Finally after a futile search for a modest apartment of her own, Betty resigned and went back South to a city where there was segregation, but where there were other educated Negroes who had their own attractive homes.

While in the North Betty B. had sat on several housing committees which, she felt, "did little more than sit." She worked hard during her years in the city to improve conditions affecting race relations but left disillusioned and disappointed. In her going the organization and the community lost a fine leader, and so ended a courageous effort on the part of the YWCA to take a forward step toward brotherhood.

Prejudice is a much used word these days, but we do not often think of its true meaning. We equate it with dislike, but it means "pre-judging," that is, judging before the facts are in —unfair treatment on any level. Is this unfair treatment the concern of Mrs. Tom Smith of Main Street or a matter for the lawmakers? Ideally it is the concern of both working together. It is on the more personal plane that we are considering it now.

According to extensive research, prejudice has its roots in childhood experience. Extreme prejudice often indicates a resentful, unhappy childhood. Selma Hirsh explained it this way: "The prejudiced were the first to admit that from their earliest beginnings they became intimate not with love, but with fear. . . . The narratives of their youth were shrill with resentment. . . . Those low in prejudice were more inclined to remember the love, affection, and understanding in their homes than the comforts they had lacked or possessed." [1]

How is the person of bitter memory to find security?

"How can he be certain that at last he 'belongs' unless he can point to many around him who do not? How can he be sure he is finally on 'the inside,' unless all around him are those he can identify as 'outsiders'?" [2]

William Van Til, a distinguished educator and expert in the field of democratic human relations, agreed that resentment

---

[1] "Fear and Prejudice," Public Affairs Pamphlet, 245, pp. 4, 5. Copyright 1957, by the Public Affairs Committee, Inc.

[2] Ibid., p. 7.

and insecurity in childhood predispose to prejudice.[3] He also pointed out that prejudice is learned, not inherited. Children sense early whom they are expected to approve and disapprove "Prejudices can be 'caught.' Often prejudices aren't taught to young people directly. They are picked up like diseases."

When the environment is such that there is little contact between the child and the minority group, according to Dr. Van Til, he can grow to adulthood with his attitude unchallenged and pass it along to his children.

Since the early climate of the home is so important in determining attitudes, those children are fortunate who grow up in homes where people of many backgrounds are made welcome, where there is an example of treating each person as an individual, and where they hear stories and read books about others to enrich their own experience.

My father, a Protestant clergyman, as a young man embarked one summer on a trip to Rome. Aboard ship he developed a severe case of typhoid fever. He was alone, with no friends on the ship or abroad. When they reached port he was taken, desperately ill, to a nursing home conducted by the Blue Nuns. Here, in the days before wonder drugs, he hovered a long time between life and death. One night when his fever was at its worst he roused and asked the nun attending him if he heard singing.

"Yes," she told him gently. "The Sisters are in the chapel praying for you."

That night the crisis passed, and the long struggle back to health began. As children we heard him tell the story of that critical night many times and, in the course of his long ministry,

[3] *Prejudiced—How Do People Get That Way*, One Nation Library series, Anti-Defamation League of B'nai B'rith, 1957.

I cannot remember hearing him make derogatory or biased comments against the Catholic faith. There was difference of opinion, yes, but respect as well. I believe that to the end of his life he could hear the chanting of the gentle Sisters, and the music lingers still in the ears of his children.

It is not always easy to establish personal contacts with those of different background, particularly in many parts of suburbia and exurbia. It is especially difficult if one's entire social activity is limited to organizations of carefully selected membership. There is more opportunity in serving on school or civic committees or joining interest groups such as those concerned with music, art, folk dancing, or "great books." The best basis for friendship is a shared enthusiasm—whether for baseball, ceramics, chamber music, or religious education. A common interest is a sounder basis for friendship than a head-on decision to make a friend of another race.

Sometimes the same lack of subtlety is apparent on committees with a determination to be broad-minded. "How nice to have a Negro on the committee," a member might say. "Let's make her chairman to show we are unprejudiced." Perhaps her experience does not qualify her to be chairman. It is more constructive to discover her special ability, which might be secretarial, and give her the post she can fill with excellence.

One of the shocking aspects of prejudice is the unexpected flashes of it that appear in groups of friends and acquaintances. An upstanding member of church and community will relate some happening with a racial slur and conclude, "Oh, well, what can you expect? After all, they are. . . ." Some charming person will tell a joke with racial sting. What does the concerned listener do in such case?

The speaker obviously would not be inclined to tell his story

99

to members of the minority he is discussing. He is talking to a group which, he assumes, feels as he does. He is apt to be surprised to find that this is not the case. Since these remarks are likely to occur in relaxed, casual conversation, it is not usually the time or place to launch into a full-dress debate. If the implication is unjust, however, the listener can quietly ask for proof or mention facts he knows to be true.

One can hardly argue with a joke, but if it is flagrantly off key a listener can say, "I don't think that's funny." Often simply refraining from an enthusiastic response serves as a gentle nudge to the better nature of the group. Queen Victoria's "We are not amused" can be implied without the majestic spoken word. The best weapons in dealing with bias are fact and tact.

Recently I had a discussion with a man who spends his entire time studying and helping to solve interracial problems as a regional director for the Anti-Defamation League of B'nai B'rith. I asked him what he would like to see church people do to help.

"Most churches," he told me, "have certain pronouncements and principles set forth by their top governing bodies. I would like to see these pronouncements reaffirmed on the local level in terms of the local situation. I should like to see church members really live their beliefs."

He said, too, that he would like to see individuals, churches, and other organizations take advantage of the many excellent booklets, films, speakers, and other program resources offered by organizations skilled in group relations. There are many organizations and religious groups working for brotherhood. Two that have particularly interesting materials are the Anti-Defamation League and the National Conference of Christians and Jews.

The latter, operating with boards composed of Catholics, Jews, and Protestants, sponsors Brotherhood Week, a religious news service, and educational workshops. It is supported by voluntary gifts and works, not as a religious, but as a civic organization with branches in many cities. The Conference offers excellent books, pamphlets, and other resources. Among them is a tiny leaflet entitled *What You Can Do for Brotherhood*, in which the wisdom of long experience is distilled into a few words. It defines brotherhood as "giving to others rights and respects you want for yourself" and lists practical suggestions for individuals, home, school, church, clubs, and business.

The Anti-Defamation League of B'nai B'rith, supported by Jewish funds, works for the same goals as the Conference but takes a stand on legal-political issues such as integration. Also its representatives are free to take part in religious and inter-faith gatherings. Among the many publications of this group is *A Primer for Parents* by Mary Ellen Goodman, a delightfully written discussion of human relations directed to parents, but with wisdom for all readers.

Another is adapted from a Presbyterian pamphlet called *Vegetables and People* and contains a questionnaire, "Are You Prejudiced?" Some of the fifteen questions are:

Do you choose your friends only from your own religious group?

Do you think a family, because of color or religion, should be deprived of the right to buy or live in any home it can afford?

Do you feel it necessary to praise members of other racial groups whenever you speak of them?

Do you frequently say "Some of my best friends are . . ."?

Do you ever say "I'm not prejudiced, but . . ."?

A Negro doctor bought a modest home in the white section

*101*

of a large city. He and his wife were attractive, educated people, but there was indignant protest up and down the street. It was a saddening experience to a clergyman who lived nearby. "Not one of the people who were objecting thought of these as *individuals*," he told me. "No one bothered to think of the man as a fine, skilled physician. He was just a black man moving in where he wasn't wanted. Things are peaceful now. They have finally accepted him, but we have a long way to go in instilling this attitude in white neighborhoods."

What can we do to fight prejudice? At long range, we can be informed about national issues and through our votes and letters make our opinions known. At medium range, we can study the housing and other problems of discrimination in our own towns and work quietly for their betterment. At close range, through our own friendships and attitudes we can realize that example is important among families and associates.

I attended a brotherhood luncheon not long ago. It was a stimulating affair with a good speaker, but the guests sat at round tables with signs giving the names of their companies or their organizations. Perhaps a few tables contained a mixture of races and faiths, but for the most part Jews sat with Jews and Gentiles with Gentiles. Wouldn't it mean more if, for instance, the guests from a Protestant woman's association arranged to share some tables with the members of a temple group? Since brotherhood means that we are all the children of one Father, surely we should sit at the same table.

Coming to know others of different backgrounds seems an adventure at first, the opening of a door to a new view, but after a bit the differences seem to fade into the background, and the person is simply another friend, an interesting individual.

Here we might turn back to Betty B. who had a certain experience recur several times with different people. Once it went like this: A name was submitted for membership in a girl's club. Betty talked to the girl and turned in her name during a meeting. As she left the room she became aware of a loud buzz of voices, and later the secretary came to her.

"We just can't accept that girl, Betty."

"Why not? She seems like a nice girl."

"But she's a Negro!"

"Well, so am I."

The young secretary looked at her with startled eyes. "But you're different."

"And that," said Betty B. patiently, "Is just because you know me."

# 11

## HOW TO HELP IN
## EVERYDAY CONTACTS

Many people can be affected by our attitudes during the course of a single day. We can leave a somber trail or a bright path of thoughtfulness. Here are two simple examples:

Millie Barnes was twenty-five minutes late for her hair appointment. This made the operator late with the next customer, and the next, and the next, who were all annoyed and delayed in keeping their own engagements. The operator tried to catch up by missing her lunch, but, by the end of the day, was tired and cross. Her comment: "I realize that things can happen to delay my customers, but why can't they let me know so I can plan?"

The only person not concerned was Millie Barnes, who did not bother to think about this widening circle of trouble.

More cheerful, was this little incident told me by a friend:

Recently our family was motoring on a busy holiday. At one point, we had to cut left into a line of traffic. We waited and waited. Finally a driver took pity on us, slowed down, and signalled us in. My husband waved, and we all beamed at him. A little later, we came to someone in the same fix, peering at that solid line on his left. My husband said we'd better give someone else a break and let him in. Then *his* passengers beamed at us. I said I wondered if this would start a chain that would go on and on."

In our activities we make many contacts, with neighbors, friends, tradesmen, canvassers, in our offices, schools, churches, local government, doctor's offices, and hospitals. We can only touch on a few of these situations, but, in all we can seek the helpful attitude.

## NEIGHBORS

A cartoon in the New Yorker once showed two Orientals talking to each other beside the Great Wall of China, which stretched far into the distance. "Good fences," one quoted, "make good neighbors."

This pithy New England saying does not mean that we should erect massive walls. The fence need not even be of the visible sort and certainly should not bar out visiting, but it should indicate respect for the neighbor's privacy. People who live close together are bound to know much about each other, but this can be ignored, forgotten or mentally marked "confidential." A young mother described an ideal neighbor this way: "I couldn't imagine a nicer person to have next door. We don't really see much of each other unless I'm hanging out clothes or working in the garden, but she's always ready to help if I need her. We've agreed on ground rules for our children, and I think I'm so lucky to have her there."

## THOSE WHO COME TO OUR DOOR

Almost anyone can be agreeable when he wants to make a good impression, but can turn a different face to those he considers less important. The people who respect all men as individuals wear their "company manners" consistently.

For many boys a paper route is the first job experience. They find it full of surprises. Listen to one informal report:

It's sure funny how much you find out about people living on the street. Mr. Jones is always crabbing if the paper isn't right on the step. Mrs. Brown never happens to have any change the day I collect. Mrs. Smith always smiles, gives me cookies if she's baking, and has the money ready. Mrs. Black called up the paper and complained the day I was late. I wish she'd had to wade through that snow! I thought I knew the people around here, but I sure know them a lot better now.

When this boy sees his customers in church he has his own ideas on their degree of godliness.

Canvassers for Red Cross, Community Chests, Planned Parenthood, or church drives also gain new and surprising glimpses of their neighbors. Often apprehensive, undertaking the calls through a sense of responsibility, they are greeted by receptions ranging from a curtly closed door to a pleasant welcome. Only those who have rung strange doorbells on a winter afternoon can understand fully how much it means to be greeted as a person, rather than a nuisance.

Not all our callers are timid and inexperienced, however. Aggressive salesmen come who will classify our reactions and use the prescribed approach for our type. How does the person of good will deal with such visitors? Many people feel they have the right to budget their expenditures without high pressure from anyone. They have encountered too many boys and girls "working for points in a contest to get to college" who are unable, upon questioning, to disclose any likely identity or destination. A severely crippled young man struggles up the walk to sell magazine subscriptions. How can one refuse? Yet he may be part of a traveling crew of handicapped young people, recruited by a selling organization for the express purpose of capitalizing on sympathy.

A Better Business Bureau executive suggests that prospective buyers of expensive items find out retail prices of comparable goods in local stores and always buy the product, not the "gimmick," whether food for a freezer or a price reduction for referral to friends. Locally based concerns tend to be more reliable, according to the Bureau.

If the householder has no interest in purchasing it is better not to admit the salesman to the house or to take his time for the sales talk at the door. This calls for firmness but can be done with courtesy. Door slamming is not indicated. A decisive "Thank you, but I'm sorry I'm not interested, good morning" should handle the situation.

What of the sectarian missionaries who brave the neighborhood dogs to ring doorbells and save souls? A few people invite them in. Some say sharply, "Not interested." I like the practice of my kindly neighbor who asks, "What can I do for you?" She listens for a moment and then explains, "I am an active member of my own church, but I will be interested in reading the literature you are giving me. Thank you for coming."

## PUBLIC SERVANTS

A school-board election took place after considerable strife and contention. The new members were elected and the defeated members gave up their seats—with not one word of thanks. They had received no payment for toiling two or three years, often far into the night, wrestling with community problems, but not one person at the meeting arose to say a word of appreciation for their efforts.

They had, however, received enough criticism during their terms to make cynics of all but selfless public servants. It seems as though citizens who give so freely of their time and effort should receive some adult equivalent of the Scout's merit badges. Lacking such visible recognition, words of thanks, either spoken in public, written in a personal letter, or in a "letter to the editor" would be appropriate and appreciated.

## TEACHERS

Miss Burns, the new third-grade teacher, did not know many people in town. She loved the children and enjoyed meeting their parents, but after a few months, she said to a friend, "Every single time I meet the parents, they say 'How is Johnny doing?' Then they talk about all his problems. Couldn't we talk about golf or fashions or books once in a while? I'm a teacher, but I'm a person too."

"The questions aren't too bad at meetings," her friend told

her. "But when they come at a party—and Johnny happens to be a real troublemaker—well, the best thing is to say, 'If you will stop in after school on Monday we can talk about it.'"

Paperwork is a big burden for today's teachers, and they appreciate having parents fill out questionnaires, sign releases, and write excuses promptly. They do not appreciate the frequent observation, "I would have guessed you were a teacher anywhere."

Gifts to teachers are discouraged in many places, but ever welcome are notes of gratitude, such as, "Our thanks to you. Through your understanding and patience Johnny has made great progress this year. We want you to know what a fine influence you have had."

Sunday-school teachers, generally not paid for their earnest efforts, give up time and trips to be faithful to their obligation. Too often parents do not bother to meet or to thank them, sometimes do not even know their names. Words of appreciation, written or spoken; offers to help or substitute; co-operation on home projects; will not only encourage the teacher, but also will make the teacher-child relationship more meaningful.

A similar situation prevails with leaders of youth organizations, such as scouts. Those in charge would prize offers of assistance, transportation, or picnic hospitality. I heard recently of a young man who had made a practice of writing a newsy letter to his former scoutmaster each year during Boy Scout Week. The letters came through four years of college, from combat areas in the Pacific, through graduate school, and, without a break, until the leader's death. His widow said no one could measure how much those letters meant. Appreciation is a rare and beautiful thing.

## CLERGYMEN

In the old tradition, when the minister came for dinner it was a stiff occasion with the best chicken elected to the platter. Today's minister would feel it more of a compliment to be included in a backyard cookout—but he does not like to be told in admiring tones, "Why, I never would have guessed you were a minister!"

Any office that sets a man apart, whether as ship's captain, general, or president, carries an inevitable measure of loneliness. This is true, too, of the clergyman and his wife. Busy as they are, they may be hungry for the refreshment of informal companionship. They particularly enjoy contacts not limited to church membership, but based instead on such common interests as camping, golf, drama, music, or flowers.

How should the pastor be addressed? If uncertain, ask him. If he is not "Dr. Brown" perhaps it will be "Pastor Brown," "Bill," or "Father Bill." His wife may be delighted to be known as "Susan." But, please, not "Reverend" or "Reverend Brown." The correct usage is either "The Reverend Mr. (William) Brown" or simply "Mr. Brown."

One of the disturbing factors of life in a manse is the ever-ringing telephone and doorbell. Parishioners can help in little ways such as replacing a telephone call with a postcard and not dropping into study or manse without prearrangement.

A minister works and prays for a troubled lot of people. He tries to give strength to the faltering and, with God's help, to solve problems that defy man. Often the results are discouraging or long delayed. One of his rewards is to discover that he has helped. Sometimes this happens a long time later, but every clergyman treasures those messages that come from down the street or across the world saying, "You'll never know how much you helped me to find the way. God bless you."

## DOCTORS

Doctors, too, appreciate words or letter of thanks from a patient they have helped—or have done all they could to help. The doctor sees many people. Unless you are personal friends he may not recall your name when you meet outside the office. It is helpful to mention it—"Good morning, Doctor, I'm Mary Jones." A common annoyance is the person who thinks the doctor is interested in his symptoms whenever they meet, even at parties. Many people who would never ask the grocer for a free pound of butter think nothing of asking for free medical advice.

Sometimes patients complain of having to wait too long in offices or that the doctor's manner is brusque. If they could glimpse the crises and strain of the doctor's previous twelve hours they might be less critical. A sick friend of mine once complained to her doctor, "I thought you would never get here." He looked at her with tired eyes and said quietly, "I was with a child dying of leukemia." No more was said, but my friend grew in understanding.

How can we be helpful in our everyday contacts? We have touched on only a few specific situations, but these and the others that mark our days, have a common denominator. Miss Burns summed it up when she said, "I am a teacher, but I'm a person too."

# 12

## HOW TO HELP
## THROUGH LISTENING

Listening is one of the finest services one person can offer another. Listening means more than merely hearing. It can be a creative attitude that enriches the joy of another's happiness and eases the ache of his trouble. This is true whether the confidant is five years old or eighty-five. Too often, unfortunately, we do not listen with warm understanding. Do these glimpses of family life sound familiar?

Junior burst through the door shouting, "Do you know what I found? A skin a snake left behind!"

The thrill and triumph are complete except for the sharing, but a tired mother responded, "Junior, you didn't wipe your feet."

"There's the neatest model plane down at the Hobby Store," Junior's brother announced at supper. "I earned enough money today to get it, and I'm going right after supper. You can help me build it, Dad."

But Dad had had a hard day and responded with no enthusiasm. "You've got a lot of algebra to do, young man."

Dad came home from work full of news. "You know, dear, Bill came into the office today. He's all steamed up about a new branch in Cleveland. This means big possibilities."

"Good," said his wife. "I rather think the hot water tank is leaking."

A friend told about a new book. "I never knew Shakespeare's time could be so fascinating. One night after his players had given a command performance of *Midsummer Night's Dream* the king was so pleased he ordered them to start right in and do *Hamlet*."

"I never could see Shakespeare. Do you think skirts will be longer this year?"

Bringing an enthusiasm, an idea, or an experience to share with another is like bringing a gift or showing a treasure. Too often the gift is rejected, leaving a hungry or bruised spirit. Janice was a mother who understood this well. A neighbor called her early one afternoon. "Come on over and have some coffee, Janice. I have some old friends here. Make it about three."

"If you don't mind I'll come later."

"Aren't your kids big enough to take care of themselves when they come home from school?"

"Yes, but I always try to be on hand when they burst in just to listen. You know a lot of wonderful things are like omelets. They won't wait! And sometimes there are troubles. I was glad I was home the day Sally burst in after a really rough day at school and said accusingly, 'Mother, you gave me the wrong sandwiches . . . and I don't believe in God!' "

Listening to good news and exciting plans calls mainly for interest and full attention. Listening to troubles calls for these and, in addition, both intuition and skill. Some troubles evaporate in the telling; some are seen in a new perspective; some indicate that expert help is needed.

Jill, aged fourteen, came home from school in a haze of gloom. She sighed frequently, was sharp with her brother and sister, setting off a train of trouble, and had little to say. Her mother, a brisk, cheerful person, did not think much of the climate Jill was creating. Although the mother had never read a book of modern psychology her instincts were sound, and she refrained from saying, "For goodness sake, Jill. Cheer up!" Instead, she left her mixing bowl, sat down with her daughter in the living room, and began to knit.

"Something is wrong, Jill. What about the play?"

"I didn't get in it."

"That's too bad, but not everyone could. You'll have another chance. What else?"

"Well, I wasn't invited to Babs' party."

"Did you expect to be?"

"Well, not exactly, but I thought maybe."

"What else?"

"One of the boys made fun of my freckles."

"Just teasing to get some attention probably. What else."

"Oh, lots of things."

"Like what?"

The conversation continued, as though the mother had nothing else to do, with each successive trouble sounding less important. When Jill couldn't think of any more her mother said sympathetically, "Well, you do seem to have a lot of problems."

Suddenly Jill giggled, her usual sunny self. "I guess they're not so bad after all. Thanks, Mom."

Many of her elderly friends come to the office of a Golden Age director to tell their troubles.

"Worries build up so, when a person is all alone. I say very little, just enough to get the story poured out. Usually by the time the problem or the fear or the grievance is talked out a person feels so much better that only in rare cases I find I should refer them for psychiatric help."

The trained counselors who deal with those whose perplexities are beyond their own handling lead their visitors to tell everything they can relating to the problem. Usually this cannot be done in one visit, but means a succession of talks as more and more details and half-forgotten memories come to the surface. In the end it is not the counselor who tells the client what course to take. The technique is to guide the troubled one to recognize his problem and to see ways to solution. In this way, self-understanding is deepened, and he is not dependent upon another for future direction.

Dealing with tangled emotions calls for much training and skill, but professional counselors are not always available, and many problems of everyday living are not urgent enough to warrant their attention. We all have the experience from time to time of having friends come to tell us their troubles and ask our help. We can learn two things from the professionals. The first is discretion and the second is to refrain from advice. Instead of giving advice, try to help the individual to solve his own problem.

Suppose a wife comes and tells in great distress how her husband has been drinking or has been going out with another woman. It is tempting to drop a few hints of this startling news to other acquaintances, but confidences such as this should be kept as inviolate as those made in a doctor's office or a priest's confessional.

A natural instinct of a sympathetic person might be to say "It's an outrage for you to be treated this way. If I were you I would tell him it's time for a showdown. He shouldn't be allowed to get away with it." The fact remains that "I" am not "you." The right and natural course for one person might spell disaster for another. Our role is to help the troubled one to get his problem crystallized, to get it out into words where he can see it and get hold of it.

Sometimes advice is sought and may be valuable, if the seeker is not looking for an easy answer. A young man might say to an older friend, "I have two mining job offers. You know a lot about this field. On the basis of your experience which do you think is most promising?"

The wise friend would discuss the trends and factors involved, but would not say, "The only course for you, my boy. . . ." He would be more likely to say, "If I were deciding, I believe the thing that would influence me is the chance of expansion in the second location. But it's your decision."

Because we are not professional counselors, there are times when an overwrought person may want to tell us more than we think we should hear, things that we sense she might regret telling later.

Linda, a very young wife, ran across the road, tears streaming down her face and knocked on her neighbor's door.

"Bob said my cooking is so terrible he's going to walk out on me. He got mad because I said I didn't have enough money to buy decent food, and he said I spent it all on other things, and I told him . . ."

"Let's have a cup of coffee, Linda. I had the kettle on anyway and was just going to turn on this new record. Sit here a minute while I get things ready."

They drank their coffee without saying very much and then Linda burst out, "What shall I do? And do you know what Bob did?"

She seemed surprised when the neighbor did not reply with a fascinated "what?"

"Look, Linda. I'm not sure you want to tell me all these things. Marriage is the private affair of two people, and you are pretty upset now. What do you think is the real cause of your quarreling? This happens to lots of couples, even when they love each other very much."

"Well . . . maybe it's because Bob wants to live an organized life, with everything neatly planned and budgeted. My father worked all over the country on construction jobs, and we lived in rented places and trailers. We never could plan much, and I guess I still just spend what I can get my hands on . . . and when he gets mad I get mad."

"But you do love Bob, I know."

Tears welled in Linda's eyes. "I love him so much it hurts every time he gets that disapproving look."

"Do you love him enough to make the kind of home he has dreamed of and is working so hard for?"

"If I only could . . . but how can I?"

"I can't tell you how, but I have a hunch that you and he can do it together. He may still act hurt when he comes back, but if you stay your best, sweet self I think you will find he wants to be happy, too. Could you tell him what you told me and ask how you can work things out together?"

"He likes to have me ask things," Linda reflected and stood up suddenly. "I think I'll go home and make a pie. Thank you for the coffee—and everything."

Skill in listening is a precious asset in family life. A mother with intuition can often pick up a signal of a forthcoming confidence and make it easier to express. Listening to a husband talk out his problems, even if they are not understood, can sometimes help him find their solution.

"I remember so clearly," the wife of a research scientist told me, "sitting and knitting while my husband paced the floor talking in chemical terms that might have come from Mars as far as I was concerned. After a while he stopped pacing and said, 'I've got it!'—and there it was."

Many a wife has listened to speeches and arguments as a trial audience. Others have won their husbands' gratitude by listening sympathetically to a tired man's silence.

Sometimes our listening ear is sought by friends with troubles so grave that we know emergency help is needed. A boy threatens suicide, a girl contemplates an abortion, a woman is in danger from a rejected suitor, a mind is torn by religious conflicts. There are many problems that cannot be resolved by sympathetic listening and a cup of coffee. With these the greatest service is to help the troubled one make contact with a wise pastor, doctor, or social worker through a family service society. This may make the difference between a restored or a shattered life.

Listening creatively can be a true gift of love.

# 13

## HELPING OTHERS TO FIND HELP

Few troubles are unique. They follow patterns which are familiar to the experts who deal with them, experts who can give special help.

Ann Landers, a gifted newspaper columnist who deals with personal problems in a style notable for both wit and compassion, was speaking one day of the great variety of troubles contained in the letters that come to her desk. She commented:

People are forever asking if the letters are genuine or whether we make them up. We couldn't if we tried. A few are hoaxes, and we develop a special intuition for these, but most are written out of a heart's agony, written because the person knows nowhere else to turn. A girl is having a baby out of wedlock, a home is racked with fighting and drunkenness, a crime has been committed, a wife is deserted, some tormented soul contemplates suicide as the only way out. What should the writer do?

Help is closer than my correspondents think. For every city where the column appears we have a complete file of social agencies. We consult this and write back telling him—or more often—her to get in touch with whichever agency can help—Salvation Army Home for unmarried mothers, Mental Health Clinic, Legal Aid, or family service society.[1]

Experience shows that help is often closer than we think. It may be a surprise to know what resources are available just a few blocks away, but many troubled people would never find this out unless some concerned friend pointed the way to the open door.

When specialized assistance is needed a clergyman or a doctor may know just where to turn. There remain, however, many situations of everyday life where sympathetic individuals, rather than organizations and specialists, can help. As friends, relatives, and neighbors, we can widen our usefulness through reading, listening, and reaching out to others. Ours is a busy time, but it is a good time to recall those challenging words of an ancient wisdom: "with all thy getting get understanding."

Several sources of help are listed below.

### Chapter 2: How to Help in Time of Sorrow

Evans, Dale. *Angel Unaware.* Westwood, N. J.: Fleming H. Revell Company, 1953.

Vining, Elizabeth Gray. *The World in Tune.* New York: Harper & Brothers, 1954.

[1] Used by permission.

## Chapter 3: HELP AND SELF-HELP FOR THE NEWCOMER

American Council for Nationalities Service, The, 20 West 40th Street, New York 18, N. Y., offers its services to immigrants, refugees, and new citizens. Most of its member agencies in forty cities are known as International Institutes.

## Chapter 4: HOW TO HELP THROUGH LETTERS

Children's Plea for Peace, World Affairs Center, University of Minnesota, Minneapolis, Minn. Ages 8-18. Enclose stamp. Good for schools, scouts, youth groups, 4-H clubs, as well as individuals.

English Speaking Union, 16 East 69th Street, New York, N. Y. Age 9-16, British Commonwealth Countries. Send stamped, self-addressed envelope and give age and hobbies.

International Friendship League, 40 Mt. Vernon Street, Boston 8, Mass. Any age. Emphasis on students and young adults. Send stamped, addressed envelope, age, hobbies.

Letters Abroad, 45 East 65th Street, New York 18, N. Y. (Adults over 15). Enclose stamped, addressed envelope.

## Chapter 5: HOW TO HELP THE HANDICAPPED

### The Deaf

Boyd, Greydon G. *Hearing Loss: What Can Be Done about It.* Philadelphia: J. B. Lippincott Company, 1959.

Davis, Hallowell, and Silverman, S. Richard (eds.). *Hearing and Deafness.* Rev. ed. New York: Holt, Rinehart & Winston, Inc., 1960.

John Tracy Clinic, 924 West 37th Street, Los Angeles, Cal., offers home study course for parents of deaf children.

Lexington School for the Deaf, 904 Lexington Avenue, New York, N. Y. Dr. Clarence D. O'Connor.

New York League for the Hard of Hearing, 480 Lexington Avenue, New York, N. Y.

## The Blind

American Foundation for the Blind, 15 West 16th Street, New York 11, N.Y. This is a clearing house for information relating to blind and deaf-blind. The Foundation publishes *Periodicals of Special Interest to Blind Persons in the United States and Canada* and lists both raised-type and talking-book items.

Bindt, Juliet. *A Handbook for the Blind.* New York: The Macmillan Company, 1952.

*Catholic Review, The.* Braille monthly published by Xavier Society for the Blind, 154 East 23rd Street, New York 10, N. Y.

*Jewish Braille Review.* Monthly published by Jewish Braille Institute of America, Inc., 48 East 74th Street, New York 21, N. Y.

John Milton Society, The. Protestant. 475 Riverside Drive, New York, N. Y., and 154 University Avenue, Toronto, Ontario.

*Science Recorded.* One tape recording monthly. Science for the Blind, Haverford College, Haverford, Pa.

Yates, Elizabeth. *The Lighted Heart.* New York: E. P. Dutton & Company, 1960.

## Chapter 6: HELPFUL ATTITUDES TOWARD ALCOHOLISM

Alateen Groups for teen-agers and Al-Anon Family Groups, P. O. Box 182, Madison Square Station, New York 10, N. Y.

Alcoholics Anonymous is listed in telephone directories and newspaper personal advertisements in most cities. Its headquarters address is Box 459, Grand Central Annex, New York 17, N. Y.

Blakeslee, Alton L. *Alcoholism—A Sickness That Can Be Beaten.* Public Affairs pamphlet, No. 118. Public Affairs Pamphlets, Inc., 22 West 38th Street, New York 16, N. Y.

Mann, Mrs. Marty. *Marty Mann's New Primer on Alcoholism.* New York: Holt, Rinehart & Winston Company, 1958.

National Council on Alcoholism, 2 East 103rd Street, New York 29, N. Y. Fifty-eight branches. This is a clearing house of scientific information and public education programs. Lists of its publications are available.

## Chapter 7: Helpful Attitudes Toward Mental Illness

Doyle, Kathleen. *When Mental Illness Strikes Your Family.* Public Affairs pamphlet, No. 172. A discussion of symptoms, admission or commitment to mental hospitals, choice of private or state hospitals, treatments, and attitudes of family.

National Association for Mental Health, 10 Columbus Circle, New York 19, N. Y.

Thorman, George. *Toward Mental Health.* Public Affairs pamphlet, No. 120.

## Chapter 8: How to Help the Aging

Collins, Thomas. "Retire and Be Rich." Golden Years Booklet, Box 1672, Grand Central Station, New York 17, N. Y.

Lawton, George, and Stewart, Maxwell S. *When You Grow Older.* Public Affairs pamphlet, No. 131.

Neisser, Edith G. *How to Be a Good Mother-in-Law and Grandmother.* Public Affairs pamphlet, No. 174.

Ogg, Elizabeth. *When Parents Grow Old.* Public Affairs pamphlet, No. 208.

## Chapter 9: How to Help with Heartaches

Buck, Pearl S. *The Child Who Never Grew.* New York: John Day Company, 1950.

MacLeish, Archibald. *J. B.* Boston: Houghton Mifflin Company, 1958.

National Association for Retarded Children, 99 University Place, New York 3, N. Y.

Paton, Alan. *Cry, the Beloved Country.* New York: Charles Scribner's Sons, 1948.

Perry, Natalie. *Teaching the Mentally Retarded Child.* New York: Columbia University Press, 1960.

## Chapter 10: How to Help Fight Prejudice

Allport, Gordon W. *The Nature of Prejudice*. Reading, Mass: Addison-Wesley Publishing Company, 1954.

Alpenfels, Ethel J. *Sense and Nonsense about Race*. New York: Friendship Press, 1946.

Anti-Defamation League of B'nai B'rith, 515 Madison Avenue, New York 22, N. Y.

Fitch, Florence Mary. *One God—The Ways We Worship Him*. Boston: Lothrop, Lee & Shepard Company, 1944.

Goodman, Mary Ellen. *A Primer for Parents*. Anti-Defamation League pamphlet, 1959.

Hirsh, Selma. *Fear and Prejudice*. Public Affairs pamphlet, No. 245.

National Conference of Christians and Jews, 43 West 57th Street, New York 19, N. Y.

Van Til, William. *Prejudiced—How Do People Get That Way?* Anti-Defamation League pamphlet and Joseph Kaplan Project in Intergroup Education, 1957.